The Open University

Mathematics Foundation Course Unit 4

FINITE DIFFERENCES

Prepared by the Mathematics Foundation Course Team

Correspondence Text 4

The Open University Press

Open University courses provide a method of study for independent learners through an integrated teaching system including textual material, radio and television programmes and short residential courses. This text is one of a series that make up the correspondence element of the Mathematics Foundation Course.

The Open University's courses represent a new system of university level education. Much of the teaching material is still in a developmental stage. Courses and course materials are, therefore, kept continually under revision. It is intended to issue regular up-dating notes as and when the need arises, and new editions will be brought out when necessary.

The Open University Press Limited
Walton Hall, Bletchley, Bucks

First Published 1970
Copyright © 1970 The Open University

Printed in Great Britain by
J W Arrowsmith Ltd

SBN 335 01003 2

Contents

Objectives

The general aim of this unit is to describe some practical methods of handling data in tabular form.

After working through this unit you should be able to:

 (i) form difference tables and use them for interpolation and extra-polation;
 (ii) explain what is meant by differencing a function, and be able to difference some elementary functions;
(iii) use difference methods to trace and correct blunders in a table of values; discuss the effects of inherent errors on difference tables; and judge how many differences may usefully be employed in the Gregory-Newton method;
(iv) explain the principle involved in polynomial interpolation;
 (v) use the Gregory-Newton formula for numerical interpolation (you will not normally be expected to work beyond the quadratic approxi-mation);
(vi) use difference methods to sum finite series of the form

$$\sum_{r=1}^{m} (a + br + cr^2)$$

where r takes integral values.

N.B.

Before working through this correspondence text, make sure you have read the general introduction to the mathematics course in the Study Guide, as this explains the philosophy underlying the whole course. You should also be familiar with the section which explains how a text is constructed and the meanings attached to the stars and other symbols in the margin, as this will help you to find your way through the text.

Structural Diagram

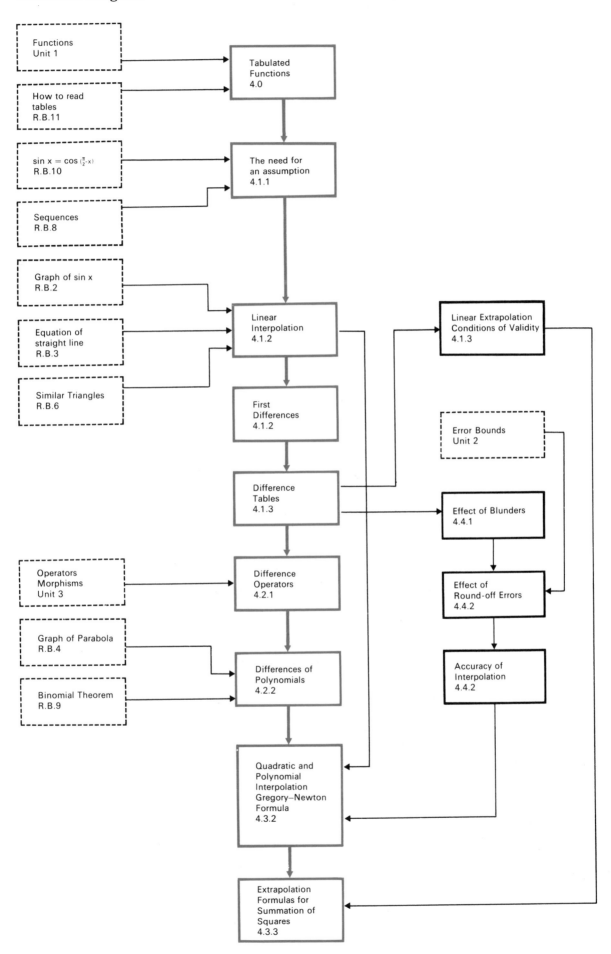

Glossary

Terms which are defined in this glossary are printed in CAPITALS.

BINOMIAL EXPANSION	The BINOMIAL EXPANSION is the POLYNOMIAL identity $$(x + h)^n = x^n + \binom{n}{1} x^{n-1}h + \binom{n}{2} x^{n-2}h^2 + \cdots + h^n$$ (See *RB 9*.)	33
COEFFICIENTS	The constants in a POLYNOMIAL are called COEFFICIENTS.	31
CONTINUOUS	The term CONTINUOUS, as applied to a function in this text, means that the graph of the function is continuous in the sense that there are no breaks or jumps in the curve. (A more rigorous definition of continuity will be given in *Unit 7, Sequences and Limits I*.)	34
CUBIC FUNCTION	A CUBIC FUNCTION is a POLYNOMIAL FUNCTION of degree 3.	30
CUBIC POLYNOMIAL	A CUBIC POLYNOMIAL is a POLYNOMIAL of degree 3.	30
DIFFERENCE OPERATOR	The DIFFERENCE OPERATOR for spacing h, denoted by Δ_h, operates on the set of all REAL FUNCTIONS, F, as follows: $$\Delta_h(f) = [x \longmapsto f(x + h) - f(x)] \quad (f \in F)$$	23
DIFFERENCE TABLE	A DIFFERENCE TABLE is a table whose first column contains the TABULAR VALUES of a TABULATED FUNCTION, and whose succeeding columns contain FIRST DIFFERENCES, SECOND DIFFERENCES, etc. The TABULAR POINTS must be evenly spaced.	18
EXTRAPOLATION	If $x_m, \ldots x_n$ are TABULAR POINTS of a TABULATED FUNCTION f, then EXTRAPOLATION is the estimation of the images under f of points outside the interval $[x_m, x_n]$, by means of a constructed function g which FITS f at the points $x_m, \ldots x_n$.	2
FINITE DIFFERENCES	FINITE DIFFERENCES is a general term applied to FIRST DIFFERENCES, SECOND DIFFERENCES, etc., and also differences $f(x_2) - f(x_1), f(x_3) - f(x_2), \ldots$, where $x_1, x_2, \ldots$ are in ascending order but not necessarily evenly spaced.	3
FIRST DIFFERENCES	If $x_1, \ldots x_n$ are evenly spaced TABULAR POINTS, with spacing h, for a TABULATED FUNCTION f, then the FIRST DIFFERENCES are the images of $x_1, \ldots x_{n-1}$, under the function $\Delta_h f$, where Δ_h is the DIFFERENCE OPERATOR for spacing h.	10
FIT	A function g FITS a function f at points $x_1, \ldots x_n$ if $g(x_k) = f(x_k)$, for $k = 1, 2, \ldots n$.	35
GREGORY-NEWTON FORMULA	The GREGORY-NEWTON FORMULA for nth degree POLYNOMIAL INTERPOLATION to the function f is $$g(x) = f(x_k) + \theta\Delta_h f(x_k)$$ $$+ \tfrac{1}{2}\theta(\theta - 1)\Delta_h^2 f(x_k) + \cdots$$ $$+ \frac{1}{n!}\theta(\theta - 1)(\theta - 2)\ldots(\theta - n + 1)\Delta_h^n f(x_k)$$ where $x_k, x_{k+1}, \ldots x_{k+n}$ are evenly spaced TABULAR POINTS, with spacing h. g FITS f at the points $x_k, \ldots x_{k+n}$.	40, 42

INTERPOLATION	If $x_m, \ldots x_n$ are TABULAR POINTS of a TABULATED FUNCTION f, then INTERPOLATION is the estimation of the images under f of certain points inside the interval $[x_m, x_n]$ by means of a constructed function g which FITS f at the points $x_m, \ldots x_n$.	2
LAGRANGE'S INTERPOLATION POLYNOMIAL	If x_k, x_{k+1}, x_{k+2} are three TABULAR POINTS of a TABULATED FUNCTION f, then the following QUADRATIC POLYNOMIAL is called LAGRANGE'S INTERPOLATION POLYNOMIAL, and FITS f at x_k, x_{k+1}, x_{k+2}	40

$$q(x) = \frac{(x - x_{k+1})(x - x_{k+2})}{(x_k - x_{k+1})(x_k - x_{k+2})} f(x_k)$$

$$+ \frac{(x - x_k)(x - x_{k+2})}{(x_{k+1} - x_k)(x_{k+1} - x_{k+2})} f(x_{k+1})$$

$$+ \frac{(x - x_k)(x - x_{k+1})}{(x_{k+2} - x_k)(x_{k+2} - x_{k+1})} f(x_{k+2})$$

LINEAR EXTRAPOLATION	LINEAR EXTRAPOLATION is EXTRAPOLATION by means of a LINEAR FUNCTION.	17
LINEAR FUNCTION	A LINEAR FUNCTION is a POLYNOMIAL FUNCTION of degree 1; i.e. a function whose graph is a straight line.	6
LINEAR INTERPOLATION	LINEAR INTERPOLATION is INTERPOLATION by means of a LINEAR FUNCTION.	10
MEAN PROPORTIONAL PARTS	MEAN PROPORTIONAL PARTS are PROPORTIONAL PARTS averaged over a group of TABULAR POINTS.	14
NEWTON-GREGORY FORMULA	See GREGORY-NEWTON FORMULA.	
nth DIFFERENCES	If $x_1, \ldots x_m$ are evenly spaced TABULAR POINTS, with spacing h, of a TABULATED FUNCTION f, and if $m > n$, then the nth DIFFERENCES are the images of $x_1, x_2, \ldots x_{m-n}$ under the function $\Delta_h^n f$, where Δ_h^n is the nth DIFFERENCE OPERATOR for spacing h.	25
nth DIFFERENCE OPERATOR	The nth DIFFERENCE OPERATOR for spacing h, denoted by Δ_h^n, operates on the set of all REAL FUNCTIONS and is the n-fold composition of the DIFFERENCE OPERATOR Δ_h with itself, i.e.	25

$$\Delta_h^n = \Delta_h \circ \Delta_h \circ \cdots \circ \Delta_h$$

PERIODIC FUNCTION	A function f with domain R is said to be PERIODIC with period h if $f(x + h) = f(x)$ for all $x \in R$, where $h \in R$ is the smallest positive number for which this equation holds.	27
POLYNOMIAL	A POLYNOMIAL of degree n in x is an expression of the form $a_n x^n + a_{n-1} x^{n-1} + \cdots + a_0$, where x is regarded as a variable, $a_n, \ldots a_0$ as constants, and $a_n \neq 0$.	31
POLYNOMIAL EXTRAPOLATION	POLYNOMIAL EXTRAPOLATION is EXTRAPOLATION by means of a POLYNOMIAL FUNCTION.	43
POLYNOMIAL FUNCTION	A POLYNOMIAL FUNCTION of degree n is a function of the form $x \longmapsto f(x)$, where $f(x)$ is a POLYNOMIAL of degree n in x, and the domain of f is R or a subset of R.	31
POLYNOMIAL INTERPOLATION	POLYNOMIAL INTERPOLATION is INTERPOLATION by means of a POLYNOMIAL FUNCTION.	39

Notation

The symbols are presented in the order in which they appear in the text.

Bibliography

L. Brand, *Differential and Difference Equations*, (John Wiley 1966).
This is an excellent reference book for differential and difference equations. Its special interest in relation to this unit is Chapter 8, "Linear Difference Equations". Chapter 13 deals with interpolation and numerical quadrature which is probably too difficult at this stage. This book is recommended to all students who are going to specialize in mathematics — both for undergraduate and post-graduate reference.

G. Boole, *A Treatise on the Calculus of Finite Differences*, (Dover Publications 1960).
This is an "old-fashioned" book, first published in 1860. Nevertheless it is a classic in the field of Finite Differences. All students are urged to have a look at this book, although because of notation etc., it will not be very useful for study.

R. Butler and E. Kerr, *An Introduction to Numerical Methods*, (Pitman 1962).
This book has many worked examples and uses a "practical" approach to interpolation which may be appreciated by newcomers to the subject.

K. L. Nielsen, *Methods in Numerical Analysis*, 2nd ed. (Collier–Macmillan, 1964).
This is a pleasantly written book on Numerical Analysis. It contains many examples, but students without previous knowledge will probably find it hard.

B. Noble, *Numerical Methods Vol. II : Differences, Integration and Differential Equations*, (Oliver and Boyd 1964).
This is a difficult book, but it contains a good discussion of interpolation.

L. J. Comrie, *Chambers's Four-Figure Mathematical Tables*, (W. and R. Chambers 1969).

This book contains very good four-figure tables of elementary functions.

4.0 INTRODUCTION

The principal aim of this unit is to tell you how to work with a function for which a number of elements of its graph have been calculated or given. The concept of a function was explained in *Unit 1, Functions*; here we are concerned with functions whose domain and codomain are both sets of real numbers (i.e. R or subsets of R). In principle, given any x belonging to the domain, it is always possible to find the image of x by applying the rule by which the function is defined. In practice, however, it may not be possible to use this method every time an image under the function is required: the rule may be too complicated to apply conveniently, or in some cases it may not even be known. In such cases it may be that the images (or even approximate values of the images) of some particular numbers $x_1, x_2, x_3, \ldots$, in the domain can be found and in this case these images can be listed together with $x_1, x_2, x_3, \ldots$, in the form of a table. Such a table is a subset of the graph of the function. The most familiar examples of such tables are the tables of logarithms and of trigonometrical functions which we learn to use at school.

Table I

x	$\log x$
1.0	0.0000
1.1	0.0414
1.2	0.0792
1.3	0.1139
1.4	0.1461
1.5	0.1761

We often face the problem of estimating images of values of x that are not tabulated: for example, can we, if necessary, obtain an accurate value of log 1.05, or of log 1.6, from the values given in Table I? This is the type of problem with which we shall deal.

For functions such as the logarithm, sine or cosine, the use of tables is a matter of convenience only: with the aid of a computer we can calculate the logarithm or sine or cosine of a number without using any tables (the way it is done will be explained in *Unit 14, Sequences and Limits II*). Many functions, however, are formed from much more complicated rules than the one defining the logarithm: an example would be the function:

$$\left\{\begin{array}{l}\text{Position on an}\\\text{aeroplane wing}\end{array}\right\} \longmapsto \left\{\begin{array}{l}\text{Net upward force on unit area}\\\text{of the wing at that position}\end{array}\right\}$$

To calculate the images under this function for a given aeroplane wing (under given conditions of flight), even at a few dozen positions on the wing, would be a major computing project, and the more positions were taken the more costly the project would be. It is therefore much more practical to tabulate the images under the function at not too many positions and use the methods of this unit to estimate the images at other positions. Thus the computer revolution has not made the techniques for working with tabulated functions (i.e. functions for which a subset of its graph is specified by a table) obsolete; rather, it has greatly extended the range of functions to which it is possible to apply them.

There are other situations too in which we may come across tabulated functions. The tabulated function may result from a sequence of experimental observations, as for example, in the tables used by engineers for designing steam engines. Here is an extract from such a table* :

Table II

Pressure (lbf/in^2)	Boiling Point of Water (°F)
300	417.33
350	431.72
400	444.59
450	456.28

In this case the function is defined by a physical relationship rather than by a mathematical one such as the logarithm, but the domain and co-domain of the function are again subsets of R, and so the method of using the table is just the same as before. An engineer who needed the boiling point of water at a pressure of say, 325 lbf/in^2 could estimate it from Table II using the same methods as one uses to estimate log 1.05 from Table I. This problem of estimating the image of a number lying between two of the tabulated numbers in the domain is called the problem of interpolation. One of the objectives of this unit is to show you accurate and convenient methods for doing interpolation.

A third type of function that can be tabulated is one that you will have come across if you have ever done an intelligence test. A simple example of a question in such a test is the following:

What is the next number in the sequence

1, 3, 5, 7, ...?

This sequence can be regarded as a list of image values of a function, call it f, where

$$f:n \longmapsto (n\text{th number in sequence}), \quad (n \in Z^+),$$

where Z^+ is the set of positive integers. It therefore corresponds to a table

n	nth number in sequence
1	1
2	3
3	5
4	7
5	?
...	...

The problem set in this intelligence test is to discover the value of $f(5)$, that is, the next entry in the table. This is a problem of a similar nature to interpolation except that the element of the domain whose image we are trying to estimate lies not between two of the tabulated values but beyond the last one tabulated. The problem of estimating the images under the function for elements of the domain outside the tabulated range is called the problem of extrapolation. Another example of ex-trapolation is the problem of obtaining log 1.6 from Table I. A second objective of this unit is to teach you how to extrapolate.

Looking at the I.Q. test question shown in Sequence (1), you probably feel that the first missing number in the sequence is 9. How did you arrive at this? You may have reasoned that the second number in the sequence is 2 greater than the first, that the third is 2 greater than the second, that

* O. W. Eshbach, *Handbook of Engineering Fundamentals*, (John Wiley 1966).

the fourth is 2 greater than the third, and hence that the fifth is probably 2 greater than the fourth. If you did reason this way, you have already grasped the basic idea of the method that gives this unit its title, namely the method of finite differences. In this method we focus attention on the differences between the successive numbers in a sequence of images under a function. These differences are called finite differences to distinguish them from other differences considered in a later unit. In this later unit, *Unit 12, Differentiation I*, we take the difference of images of numbers in the domain that are allowed to be arbitrarily close together, whereas in the subject of finite differences, the difference between them is kept fixed. Because of the link with differentiation, your study of finite differences in the present unit will provide you with a useful introduction to some of the ideas of *Differentiation I* and the other units on calculus, while avoiding for the present the extra conceptual apparatus (the concept of limit) that is needed to deal with quantities that are allowed to be arbitrarily close together.

Definition 3
* *

Since digital computers are well suited to finite differences, there are processes which used to be calculated using calculus and are now, in some cases, calculated with the aid of finite differences.

4.1 LINEAR INTERPOLATION AND EXTRAPOLATION

4.1

4.1.1 The Need for an Assumption

4.1.1

Every method of interpolation or extrapolation depends on an assumption about the nature of the function that has been tabulated. For example, in the I.Q. test question we have already mentioned:

"What is the next number in the sequence

Discussion
* *

$$1, 3, 5, 7, \ldots?"$$

Sequence (1)

the obvious answer is 9, since the numbers appear to be formed from the rule: "to find the next number, add 2"; in other words they form an arithmetic progression (sequence)

$$a, a + d, a + 2d, a + 3d, \ldots$$

Sequence (2)

with $a = 1$ and $d = 2$. But is it really as simple as that? Why shouldn't the answer be 11? The numbers given in Sequence (1) might be the first four in a longer sequence that continues:

$$1, 3, 5, 7, 11, 13, 15, 17, 21, 23, 25, 27, 31, \ldots$$

Sequence (3)

Just by looking at the four numbers $1, 3, 5, 7$, we have no way of telling whether they come from the arithmetic sequence (2), or from the more complicated sequence (3). It is thought, both by the setters of intelligence tests and by those who have the misfortune to have to answer them, that the "reasonable" choice is the arithmetic sequence, perhaps on some such ground as that the only numbers appearing in the rule determining it can be found from the given numbers $1, 3, 5, 7$. But can we be sure that there would in every case be just one "reasonable" choice?

This problem typifies a situation that we shall meet again and again in this unit. In order to do an interpolation or (as here) an extrapolation, it is necessary first to find a simple function that has the same image values as the tabulated function at the tabulated elements in the domain. In the intelligence test example, there is a fair chance of guessing the unique function that the test setter happened to have in mind, but in general, since the whole point of the interpolation is often to approximate a complicated function by a simpler one, there will be no unique way of choosing the simple function.

The following example should help to clarify the last sentence.

Example 1 **Example 1**

A part of a table for the sine function

$$x \longmapsto \sin x \quad (x \in R)$$

is shown below.

x	$\sin x$
-0.4	-0.39
-0.3	-0.30
-0.2	-0.20
-0.1	-0.10
0	0
0.1	0.10
0.2	0.20
0.3	0.30
0.4	0.39

(The values of x are given in radians and the corresponding images are given to two significant figures.)

Now, it would seem reasonably clear that for any element in the restricted domain $[-0.4, 0.4]$, the function $x \longmapsto x$ has approximately the same image as $x \longmapsto \sin x$. Therefore, if we were only interested in this restricted domain for the sine function, we could safely *approximate the complicated function*

$$x \longmapsto \sin x \qquad (x \in [-0.4, 0.4])$$

by the simple function

$$x \longmapsto x \qquad (x \in [-0.4, 0.4])$$

However, as we said above, this approximation is not unique: for instance, you will find that both

$$x \longmapsto \cos\left(\frac{\pi}{2} - x\right) \quad (x \in [-0.4, 0.4])$$

and

$$x \longmapsto x - \frac{x^3}{6} \qquad (x \in [-0.4, 0.4])$$

are also approximations to the sine mapping with this restricted domain (the first happens to be exact, in that $\cos\left(\frac{\pi}{2} - x\right) = \sin x, (x \in R)$). The non-uniqueness is not something we can get rid of, as you can readily appreciate by considering attaching precise meanings to "complicated", "simple" and "approximate". ∎

As a consequence of the non-uniqueness, there are different methods of interpolation and extrapolation, which may well yield different results. There is no absolute criterion for choosing between these methods, except that, when the result is to be applied to, say, an engineering construction, we have a criterion of sorts: does it work? All that can be done is to use whatever information we have about the source of the tabulated numbers and to choose the new function in the simplest way that is likely to yield a good approximate representation of the original function. In order to make a good choice it is important to be able to estimate the error in an interpolation or extrapolation method. Later in the unit we shall discuss briefly how this can be done.

We have mentioned that it is important to know where the tabulated numbers come from. The most important use of this information is to tell us whether the tabulated function is sufficiently regular to justify applying interpolation or extrapolation methods at all. In the introduction we mentioned several examples of such "regular" functions: the logarithm, two functions arising in engineering, and a sequence of numbers in an intelligence test. There are, however, functions whose behaviour is much less regular and for which the methods described in this unit are not normally suitable. These are functions in which a large unpredictable or chance element takes a part. An extreme example is the sequence of numbers obtained by throwing a die or spinning a roulette wheel a large number of times. Here (fortunately for the casino owners) even the most sophisticated extrapolation techniques will not help you to predict the next number in the sequence.

Perhaps the word "predict" as used above needs qualifying. If we throw an unbiassed die, we can be certain that we shall get one of the results 1, 2, 3, 4, 5 or 6, and in a large number of throws any repeated guess of one of these six numbers would be right roughly one time in six. But this is not the same as saying that if the first seven throws give the sequence

$$6, 3, 6, 2, 1, 4, 4$$

then the next throw will give a 5. There is no law governing this sequence: each of the six numbers is equally likely to occur at the next throw. This and other similar types of sequence can be loosely classified as "statistical sequences". Finite difference methods of interpolation and extrapolation cannot be applied to this type of sequence. They are inappropriate, because to use these methods we have to make some assumption about the rule of formation of the sequence. By the very nature of the randomness implied in throwing a die, we cannot make this type of assumption for statistical sequences. We shall return to the study of this type of sequence in *Unit 16, Probability and Statistics I*.

Statistical sequences of a less extreme type are supplied by economic data such as quarterly trade figures, or stock exchange prices. For example, here is a table of the price of shares in Consolidated Gold Fields during the week 9th–16th August 1968:

	Day	Price	Change
Fri	9th August	66/6	
Mon	12th August	68/–	+1/6
Tues	13th August	69/–	+1/–
Wed	14th August	70/–	+1/–
Thur	15th August	72/–	+2/–
Fri	16th August	74/–	+2/–

The art of making money on the Stock Exchange is the art of predicting the behaviour of a sequence like the one in the table; but although the numbers in the table are not random like the ones given by casting a die, it is hardly possible to predict the sequence by finite difference methods. The numbers in the "change" column (what we are calling "differences" in this unit) are all at least 1/–, which might lead one to expect that the numbers would continue to increase steadily, perhaps by a further 5 to 10 shillings in the next week. In fact, at the end of the next week the price was the same as on the 16th, and by the end of the following week it was back to 69/-. Regrettably, we cannot promise you that a study of this unit will help you to make your fortune on the Stock Exchange. This is because share prices are determined by many other factors besides the ones shown in the table. Of course there are "trends", but these can only be identified reliably by other methods; we shall return to this question in the units on probability and statistics.

The main conclusion to be drawn from the discussion in this section is that interpolation and extrapolation methods work best when the table of numbers under consideration comes from a well-defined mathematical or empirical function which may be expected to lead to a fairly regular pattern of variation in the image values. We begin by looking at some cases where this pattern is simple enough to be approximated by a linear function, that is, one whose graph is a straight line. One example which we assumed to be of this type has already been considered: the extrapolation of the sequence 1, 3, 5, 7, ... for which the relevant function

Definition 1
* *

$$k \longmapsto (k\text{th number in sequence})$$

has the following graph:

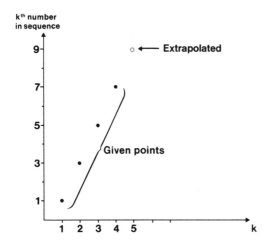

In the next section we shall consider the corresponding interpolation method.

Exercise 1

Write a paragraph discussing the applicability of Finite Difference methods to the following tabulated data.

Chemical Element	Atomic Number	Atomic Weight
. . .	. . .	. . .
Manganese	25	54.93
Iron	26	55.85
Cobalt	27	58.94
Nickel	28	58.69
Copper	29	63.54
Zinc	30	65.38
. . .	. . .	. . .

Pitch of Musical Note	Vibration Frequency *
Middle C	256
D	288
E	320
F	$341\frac{1}{3}$
G	384
A	$426\frac{2}{3}$
B	$490\frac{2}{3}$
C	512

Thousands of men under arms: Army, Navy and Air Force†

Year	Britain	France	Russia	U.S.A.	Germany	Italy
1914	397	834	1254	165	864	345
1924	349	835	678	251	114	359
1932	316	690	562	237	114	324
1939	460	864	2269	334	1182	1077
1949	770	589	4000	1616	—	?
1955	803	950	4500	2935	—	?

* Sir James Jeans, *Science and Music*, (Cambridge University Press 1961).
† P. J. Noel-Baker, *The Arms Race*, (Oceana Publications 1956).

Solution 1

For each of the three tables your answer should consider these questions:

(i) Are the tabulated values (elements of the codomain of some unspecified function) determined by the tabular points (elements of the domain of this function) in accordance with some mathematical, scientific, or other natural law, or are they significantly affected by other factors (including chance)?

(ii) If the answer to (i) is that they are determined in accordance with some law, is this law simple and regular enough for us to approximate it by a simple mathematical expression obtained from the numbers in the table?

In the chemical example, there is undoubtedly a scientific law, *but* it is not regular enough to justify the use of finite difference methods (notice how the atomic weights mostly increase with atomic number, but slip back between Cobalt and Nickel). In the musical example, the frequencies of vibration are determined by the notes in accordance with acoustical laws, *and* the law is regular enough to justify using finite difference methods; in fact, since the invention of the equally tempered scale (which is a good approximation to the diatonic scale given in the exercise), the standard method of tuning a piano has been based on a simple mathematical formula (each semitone corresponds to a factor of $\sqrt[12]{2}$ or 1.059, in frequency). In the military example, the size of a country's armed forces is undoubtedly influenced by factors other than the mere passage of time and the sizes of other countries' armed forces; and so the table (like the table of share prices in the text) does not give enough information to justify the use of finite difference methods; question (ii) does not apply in this last case. ■

4.1.2 Linear Interpolation

The simplest method of interpolation is one that is widely used in tables of elementary functions, such as log tables. In the introduction to this unit, for example, we mentioned the problem of finding log 1.05 from the following table:

Table I

x	$\log x$
1.0	0.0000
1.1	0.0414
1.2	0.0792
1.3	0.1139
1.4	0.1461
1.5	0.1761

Since 1.05 is half way between 1.00 and 1.10, the simplest estimate is to assume that log 1.05 is half way between log 1.00 and log 1.10, that is

$$\log 1.05 \simeq \frac{0.0000 + 0.0414}{2} = 0.0207$$

Equation (1)

This agrees to 3 decimal places with the value 0.0212 given in four-figure log tables. (This latter value is itself correct only to 4 decimal places; the exact value of log 1.05 is a non-terminating decimal.) In a similar way, to find log 1.13, since 1.13 is $\frac{3}{10}$ of the way from 1.10 to 1.20, the simplest estimate is log 1.10 plus $\frac{3}{10}$ of the distance to be covered in going from log 1.10 to log 1.20, that is

$$\log 1.13 \simeq \log 1.10 + \tfrac{3}{10}(\log 1.20 - \log 1.10)$$

$$= 0.0414 + \tfrac{3}{10}(0.0792 - 0.0414)$$

$$= 0.0527$$

Equation (2)

This agrees to 3 decimal places with the value 0.0531 given in four-figure tables.

The method used in deriving Equations (1) and (2) is sometimes called the method of proportional parts, since the number on the right-hand side of Equation (2) divides the interval [log 1.10, log 1.20] in the same proportion that the number 1.13 divides the interval [1.10, 1.20]. To

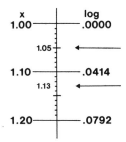

deal with the general case, let us denote the tabulated function by f and the numbers in the domain for which it is tabulated by $x_1, x_2, \ldots x_n$, arranged in increasing order. These are known as tabular points. The images of these points are then $f(x_1), f(x_2), \ldots, f(x_n)$; they are called tabular values of the function. For brevity we shall denote the tabular values by $y_1, y_2, \ldots, y_n$:

x	$f(x)$
x_1	$y_1 = f(x_1)$
x_2	$y_2 = f(x_2)$
$\ldots$	$\ldots$
x_n	$y_n = f(x_n)$

To estimate $f(x)$ when x lies between the two tabular points x_1 and x_2 say, we find the proportion in which the number x divides the interval $[x_1, x_2]$ and find the number y that divides the interval $[y_1, y_2]$ in the same proportion. We can represent the procedure graphically:

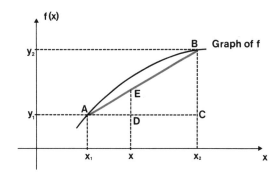

The proportion in which the number x divides the interval $[x_1, x_2]$ is

$$\frac{x - x_1}{x_2 - x_1} = \frac{AD}{AC}$$

Using the fact that triangles ADE and ACB are similar, we have

$$\frac{AD}{AC} = \frac{DE}{CB}$$

Since CB is the length of the interval $[y_1, y_2]$, E is the point whose y-coordinate divides the interval $[y_1, y_2]$ in the required proportion. So we see that our method of estimating $f(x)$ between A and B is to approximate its graph by a straight line between the two points. For this reason this method is called linear interpolation.

Some published tables give a little help in the method of linear interpolation by printing the values of $y_{k+1} - y_k$ to the right of the values of y_k and y_{k+1}, and on a line halfway between them, as for example in the following extract from a table of reciprocals:

x	$1/x$	
1.60	0.6250	
		-39
1.61	0.6211	
		-38
1.62	0.6173	
		-38
1.63	0.6135	

The numbers -39, -38, -38, known as first differences, should really be -0.0039, -0.0038, -0.0038, but they are usually printed as shown (or even without the minus sign) to save space.

Exercise 1

Use linear interpolation to obtain approximate values for

(i) log 1.25, using Table I in Section 4.1.2;
(ii) the boiling point of water at a pressure of 365 lbf/in^2 from the following table

Pressure (lbf/in^2)	Boiling Point of Water (°F)
300	417.33
350	431.72
400	444.59
450	456.28

■

The method of linear interpolation can be applied to any table whatever, but only in suitable cases can we rely on the values so obtained. The criterion is that the graph of the function should be approximately straight between the tabular points.

Exercise 2

Tabulate the values of sin x for $x = 0$, π, 2π, 3π radians, and calculate a value of $\sin \dfrac{\pi}{10}$ by linear interpolation. What do you conclude?   ■

Exercise 3

(i) Tabulate the values of sin x for $x = 0, \dfrac{\pi}{4}, \dfrac{\pi}{2}, \dfrac{3\pi}{4}$ and π, and calculate a value for $\sin \dfrac{\pi}{10}$ by linear interpolation.

(ii) Calculate a value for $\sin \dfrac{\pi}{10}$ by linear interpolation from the table at the right.

x	$\sin x$
0	0
$\dfrac{\pi}{16}$	0.1951
$\dfrac{2\pi}{16}$	0.3827
$\dfrac{3\pi}{16}$	0.5555
$\dfrac{4\pi}{16}$	0.7071

(iii) To four places of decimals, the value of $\sin \dfrac{\pi}{10}$ is 0.3090. What do you conclude by comparing this with the results of the preceding exercise and (i) and (ii) of the present exercise?   ■

Solution 1

Solution 1

(i) 0.0966

(ii) 435.58 °F.

■

Solution 2

Solution 2

x	0	π	2π	3π
$\sin x$	0	0	0	0

Linear interpolation gives $\sin \dfrac{\pi}{10} = 0$. Indeed, linear interpolation gives $\sin x = 0$ for all values of x between 0 and 3π. The conclusion is that linear interpolation can give wildly inaccurate results if the interval of tabulation is too large. One may conclude also that extreme care must be taken in cases where little is known about the function being tabulated.

■

Solution 3

Solution 3

(i)

x	$\sin x$
0	0.0000
$\dfrac{\pi}{4}$	0.7071
$\dfrac{\pi}{2}$	1.0000
$\dfrac{3\pi}{4}$	0.7071
π	0.0000

The interpolated value for $x = \dfrac{\pi}{10}$ is $0.0000 + (0.7071 - 0.0000)\theta$, with

$$\theta = \frac{\dfrac{\pi}{10} - 0}{\dfrac{\pi}{4} - 0} = \frac{4}{10},$$

$$= 0.0000 + 0.7071 \times \frac{4}{10} = 0.2828$$

(ii) The interpolated value for $x = \dfrac{\pi}{10}$ is

$$\sin\left(\frac{\pi}{16}\right) + \left[\sin\left(2\frac{\pi}{16}\right) - \sin\left(\frac{\pi}{16}\right)\right]\theta$$

with

$$\theta = \frac{\dfrac{\pi}{10} - \dfrac{\pi}{16}}{\dfrac{2\pi}{16} - \dfrac{\pi}{16}} = \frac{6}{10}$$

$$= 0.1951 + \left[0.1876 \times \frac{6}{10}\right] = 0.3077$$

(iii) The interpolated values get closer to the exact four-figure value as we reduce the interval between the tabular points.

■

Exercise 2 illustrates a case where linear interpolation is completely inappropriate: the sine function cannot be satisfactorily represented by a straight line joining tabular points as far apart as 0 and π, as is obvious from the figure.

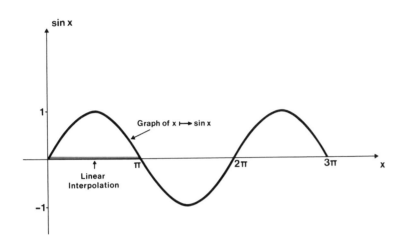

On the other hand, Exercise 3 shows two cases where the tabular points are closer together and where linear interpolation gives fairly good results. In (i) the spacing between tabular points is $\frac{\pi}{4}$, and the interpolation is in error by $0.3090 - 0.2828 = 0.0262$; in (ii) the interval width is only $\frac{\pi}{16}$ and the interpolation is in error by only $0.3090 - 0.3077 = 0.0013$. Thus, in this example, the accuracy of linear interpolation is generally better, the closer together the tabular points. This is illustrated in the figure.

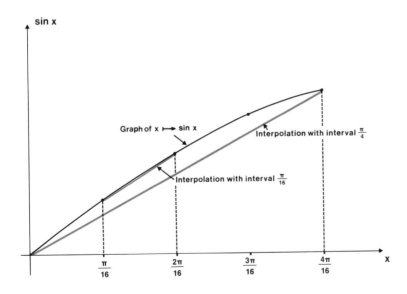

13

In designing mathematical tables such as log tables the tabular spacing is usually chosen small enough to make the error in linear interpolation no greater than the round-off error in the tabulated figures. This implies that a higher accuracy in the tables demands a smaller tabular spacing and hence more tabular entries. For example, in *Chambers's Four-Figure Tables* the logarithms occupy 4 pages, but in *Chambers's Six-Figure Tables*, (100 times as accurate), they occupy 26 pages. In four-figure tables it is customary to make the interpolation more convenient, at some cost in accuracy, by replacing the proportional parts by mean proportional parts, which are simply proportional parts averaged over a group of tabular intervals (instead of taking the nearest tabular points).

For example, in the table of reciprocals on page 15, the mean proportional part under the number 2 in the table is obtained as

$$\frac{(5882 - 6250)}{10} \times \frac{2}{10} = -\frac{736}{100} \simeq -7$$

(The minus sign is not shown in the table for brevity; you are expected to remember to subtract, since $\frac{1}{x}$ decreases as x increases.)

So whether you are reading the reciprocal of 16.12 or of 16.72 you use the same mean proportional part, i.e. -7. Whereas, if you were to use the nearest tabulated points, you would use linear interpolation on the tabulated values at 16.1 and 16.2 for 16.12, obtaining the true proportional part, $0.2(6173 - 6211) = -8$, rather than -7, and on the tabulated values at 16.7 and 16.8 for 16.72, obtaining the true proportional part $0.2(5952 - 5988) = -7$.

Exercise 4

Using the table of reciprocals, read off the reciprocals of 1.66 and 1.67 (in such tables you are often expected to find the position of the decimal point for yourself). By linear interpolation, obtain a value for the reciprocal of 1.667. Also obtain a value for the reciprocal using the mean proportional parts shown, and explain any discrepancy. ■

Discussion
* *

Definition 5
* *

Exercise 4
(5 minutes)

Table of Reciprocals

x	0	1	2	3	4	5	6	7	8	9
16	6250	6211	6173	6135	6098	6061	6024	5988	5952	5917
17	5882	...								

Mean Proportional Parts

1	2	3	4	5	6	7	8	9
4	7	11	15	18	22	26	30	33

Solution 4 **Solution 4**

$$1/1.66 = 0.6024, \quad 1/1.67 = 0.5988$$

Linear interpolation

$$1/1.667 \simeq 0.6024 + (0.5988 - 0.6024)\theta$$

with

$$\theta = \frac{1.667 - 1.66}{1.67 - 1.66} = \frac{7}{10}$$

so that $1/1.667 \simeq 0.6024 - 0.0036 \times \dfrac{7}{10} = 0.5999$

Mean proportional parts

$$1/1.667 \simeq 0.6024 - 0.0026 = 0.5998$$

(Mean proportional part for $\theta = \frac{7}{10}$ is shown in the table as 26.)

The results obtained using mean proportional parts are slightly inaccurate because the proportional parts for $\frac{7}{10}$ vary between

$$(6250 - 6211) \times \tfrac{7}{10} = 27$$

and

$$(5952 - 5917) \times \tfrac{7}{10} = 24$$

across the table, so that using the mean value 26 can introduce an error of up to 2 digits in the last decimal place. ∎

4.1.3 Extrapolation

The most important thing to know about extrapolation is that it may be considerably less accurate than interpolation. For linear extrapolation this can be seen from the figure below, which shows the graph of a function together with the straight line crossing it at two tabular points x_k and x_{k+1}. For values of x within the interval $[x_k, x_{k+1}]$, this straight line corresponds to the interpolation formula given in the preceding section and can be quite accurate if the interval is not too wide. If, however, the straight line is used for extrapolation, that is outside this interval, the accuracy falls away rapidly.

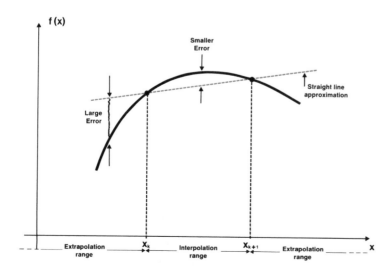

For this reason, if there is a choice between interpolation and extrapolation, interpolation is always preferable. Sometimes, however, we cannot avoid an extrapolation. This can occur, for example, if we are calculating successive entries in a table of some new function, and we need a rough estimate of the next entry in the table to use as the first approximation in an iterative process for calculating it accurately. This is the problem we shall consider here: given an incomplete table of a function, to estimate the next entry in the table.

We have already considered one problem of this type, the intelligence test question of guessing the next number in the sequence $1, 3, 5, 7, \ldots$. The method by which you solved this problem can be systematized by tabulating the sequence and recording the differences of successive tabular values just as in printed tables laid out for linear interpolation:

k	kth number in sequence	
1	1	
2	3	2
3	5	2
4	7	2
5	9	2

The column of 2's comprises the differences of successive numbers in the sequence. The natural way to continue this column is to insert a further 2; this implies that the next entry in the sequence should be a 9. This is an example of linear extrapolation, a process which can be used whenever the entries in the column of differences are all the same.

Definition 1
* * *

Exercise 1

Exercise 1
(2 minutes)

Use linear extrapolation to find estimates for the missing tabular values in the following table.

x	$\sin x$
29° 54′	
30°	0.5000
30° 6′	0.5015
30° 12′	0.5030
30° 18′	0.5045
30° 24′	

■

A less trivial extrapolation problem is provided by the table of stopping distances printed in the back of the *Highway Code*:

Main Text
* * *

Table I

Speed (mile/h)	Stopping Distance (ft)
20	40
30	75
40	120
50	175
60	240

(*continued on page 18*)

Solution 1

Linear extrapolation gives sin (30° 24′) = 0.5060 and sin (29° 54′) = 0.4985.

∎

(continued from page 17)

Suppose your driving test examiner had asked you the stopping distance for 70 mile/h, or for 10 mile/h. Here is a way to *estimate* them. Once again we form the column of differences

40	
75	35
120	45
175	55
240	65

This time the differences are not equal, but it is fairly easy to guess the next entry in the column of differences, and so to complete the solution.

Exercise 2

What is the stopping distance for a speed of 70 mile/h? ∎

(The answer to this exercise is contained in the text which follows.)

The differences in Table II form an arithmetic sequence with common difference 10; therefore the natural way to continue the difference column is to make the next entry 75. Then the next entry in the stopping-distance column must be 315, since $315 - 240 = 75$. The process by which we obtained 75 as the next entry in the difference column can be systematized by constructing a further column of numbers, the differences of successive entries in the difference column. These are called the second differences of the original sequence of stopping distances. With the second differences included the table looks like this

Table III

Speed	Stopping Distance	First Differences	Second Differences
20	40		
30	75	35	
40	120	45	10
50	175	55	10
60	240	65	10
70	315	75	10

Since the second differences of the given numbers are all 10, we expect the next entry in the second difference column also to be 10 and the other red figures are then determined by solving the equations

$$75 - 65 = 10 \quad \text{and} \quad 315 - 240 = 75$$

The array of numbers in the last three columns of Table III is called a difference table. ∎

Exercise 3

Use the *Highway Code* figures to estimate stopping distances for speeds of 80, 10 and 0 mile/h. ■

Exercise 3
(2 minutes)

Exercise 4

Here is part of a table of squares. Form a difference table for it and hence estimate 37^2 by extrapolation.

x	x^2
31	961
32	1024
33	1089
34	1156
35	1225
36	1296
37	?

■

Exercise 4
(2 minutes)

Exercise 5

The images under a function f are tabulated for equally spaced values of the variable. If the second differences are

(i) all zero,
(ii) not all zero,

what can you deduce about the graph of the function? ■

Exercise 5
(5 minutes)

Exercise 6 (Omit if you got Exercise 5 completely right).

Tabulate the images under the function

$$x \longmapsto x + \sin \pi x \quad (x \in R)$$

for $x = 0, 1, 2, 3$, and compute the second differences of this table. Evaluate the images also for $x = \frac{1}{2}, \frac{3}{2}, \frac{5}{2}$, and hence sketch the graph of the function. This is an example of a table with zero second differences from a function that is not linear. ■

Exercise 6
(3 minutes)

Solution 3 **Solution 3**

From the table we obtain the following estimates:
at 80 mile/h estimated stopping distance is 400 feet.
at 10 mile/h estimated stopping distance is 15 feet.
at 0 mile/h estimated stopping distance is 0 feet. ■

Solution 4 **Solution 4**

x	x^2	First Differences	Second Differences
31	961		
32	1024	63	
33	1089	65	2
34	1156	67	2
35	1225	69	2
36	1296	71	2
37	1369	73	2

■

Solution 5 **Solution 5**

(i) The points on the graph corresponding to tabular points in the domain lie on a straight line, but the graph itself need not be a straight line.
(ii) The graph is not a straight line. ■

Solution 6 **Solution 6**

x	$x + \sin \pi x$	First Differences	Second Differences
0	0		
1	1	1	
2	2	1	0
3	3	1	0
$\frac{1}{2}$	1.5		
$\frac{3}{2}$	0.5		
$\frac{5}{2}$	3.5		

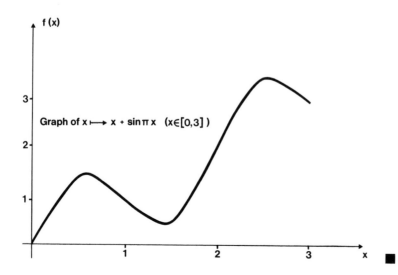

Graph of $x \longmapsto x + \sin \pi x$ $(x \in [0,3])$

■

4.1.4 Summary

In this part we have shown that the images of a tabulated function, corresponding to values between known tabular values, can be conveniently calculated using linear interpolation, provided that within the interval being used for interpolation the graph of the function is reasonably close to a straight line. Images corresponding to values outside the tabular points can also be found in a similar way, but extrapolation can be dangerous unless we have some knowledge of the function outside the tabulated range.

4.2 DIFFERENCE TABLES AND OPERATORS

4.2.0 Introduction

We saw in the preceding section that both for interpolation and for extrapolation it was useful to attach a difference table (that is, one or more columns of differences) to the tabulated values of a sequence or function. For linear interpolation and extrapolation the difference table need only include the first differences of the tabular values of the sequence or function, but when linear methods are not sufficiently accurate because the graph of the function is not a straight line, (as in the *Highway Code* example used in the preceding section; see also Exercise 4.1.3.5 (i)), we may need to include in the table columns of second differences, and perhaps also third differences (the differences of successive entries in the second-difference column), or differences of even higher order. The usefulness of difference tables is by no means confined to extrapolation. We also use them for interpolation; the resulting methods are capable of higher accuracy than the linear interpolation method discussed earlier. They make this possible because the second differences, by showing how fast the first differences are changing as we move along the table, give an indication of the deviation of the graph from a straight line (see figure) and can be used to correct for this deviation.

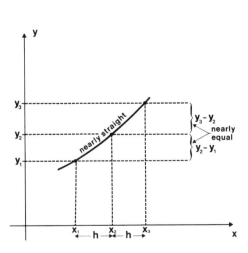

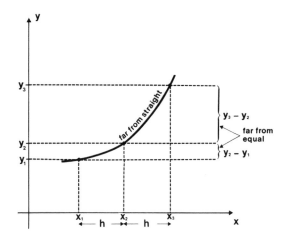

Non-linear interpolation will be considered in Section 4.3 of this unit.

A further application of the difference table that is sometimes useful is to detect a blunder in the tabulated values of the function. This application will be considered in Section 4.4 of this unit.

Before we can deal with either of these applications, however, we shall need to look into the structure of the difference table itself in more detail.

4.2.1 The Difference Operator

The structure of the difference table is determined by two factors: how the original tabular values are constructed, and how the difference table is built up from these tabular values. We consider the original tabular values first. These are the images of the tabular points $x_1, x_2, \ldots, x_n$ under the given function f. Up to now the tabular points have been ordered only by magnitude. Now, to simplify the theory, we shall make explicit a requirement that was in fact satisfied in all the examples we have considered: that is, that the tabular points be equally spaced. The spacing between the tabular points can be any positive number; it is usually denoted by h (another way of saying this is that the first differences of the sequence of tabular points are all equal to h). With this simplification, both the tabular points and the tabular values are formed by applying definite mappings to tabular points, and we have the structure shown below, where the horizontal arrows indicate an application of the function f, and the vertical arrows indicate an application of the function

$$\text{add } h : x \longmapsto x + h \quad (x \in R)$$

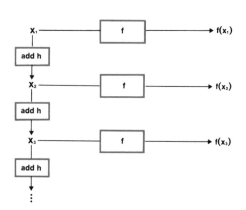

The second factor determining the structure of the difference table is the method of forming the table itself by repetitions of a single basic binary operation; this operation is to subtract two successive entries in a column and enter the result at the right, as shown in the next diagram.

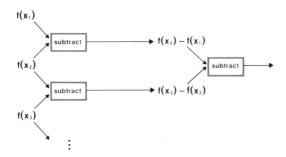

This diagram provides a description of the structure of any difference table; the basic operation it uses is a binary operation, acting on two numbers in the table.

In the case we are considering here, with the tabular points equally spaced, there is another way of looking at the columns of differences. To do this we make use of the fact that $x_2 - x_1 = h$, $x_3 - x_2 = h$, etc., so that the above diagram can be reconstructed as

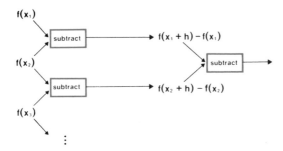

This representation shows that the column of first differences of f can be regarded as a table of the new function

$$x \longmapsto f(x + h) - f(x) \quad (x \in R)$$

with the same tabular points $x_1, x_2, \ldots$.

Here we have an operator of the type discussed in Section 1.1.7 of *Unit 1*, *Functions*. It takes any function f with domain in R and maps it to the new function defined above. Since for given h the new function is uniquely determined by f, the operator is a function whose domain is itself a set of functions: the set of all functions with domain and codomain both in R. This operator will be denoted by Δ_h, and is called the difference operator for the spacing h. The formula defining the difference operator is

Definition 1
* * *

$$\Delta_h : f \longmapsto [x \longmapsto f(x + h) - f(x)(x, x + h \in \text{domain of } f)] \quad (f \in F)$$

Notation 1

where F stands for the set of all real functions. (We define a real function to be a function whose domain and codomain are sets of real numbers.) If we omit the domain of the image function for brevity, this formula can be written more simply as

Definition 2
* *

$$\Delta_h : f \longmapsto [x \longmapsto f(x + h) - f(x)] \quad (f \in F)$$

Notation 2

An alternative way to state the definition of Δ_h is to specify the image of any element f in its domain:

$$\Delta_h(f) = [x \longmapsto f(x + h) - f(x)] \quad (f \in F)$$

Notation 3

where again the domain of the image function is omitted for brevity.

Example 1

Example 1

Consider

$$f : x \longmapsto 1 + 2x + x^2 \quad (x \in R)$$

We wish to find $\Delta_{0.2}(f)$. Note that we have now specified h, i.e. $h = 0.2$. Therefore

$$f(x + h) = f(x + 0.2) = 1 + 2(x + 0.2) + (x + 0.2)^2$$

It follows that

$$\Delta_{0.2}(f) = [x \longmapsto \{1 + 2(x + 0.2) + (x + 0.2)^2\}$$

$$- \{1 + 2x + x^2\}]$$

$$= [x \longmapsto 0.4x + 0.44] \qquad \blacksquare$$

Exercise 1

If f_1, f_2, f_3, are defined by

$$f_1 : x \longmapsto 2x \quad (x \in R)$$

$$f_2 : x \longmapsto x^2 \quad (x \in R)$$

$$f_3 : x \longmapsto 1 \quad (x \in R)$$

find $\Delta_5(f_1)$, $\Delta_{0.7}(f_2)$, and $\Delta_{0.01}(f_3)$. $\qquad \blacksquare$

The operator Δ_h maps the original tabulated function f to $\Delta_h(f)$, and the images of $x_1, x_2, \ldots$ under $\Delta_h(f)$ are tabulated in the column of first differences. By a second application of Δ_h we can obtain the function $\Delta_h(\Delta_h(f))$; the images of $x_1, x_2, \ldots$ under this function are tabulated in the column of second differences.

Our previous diagrammatic form of the difference table now becomes

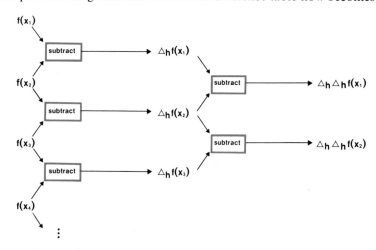

Using the notation for composition of functions introduced in Section 1.2.2 of *Unit 1, Functions*, we can write $\Delta_h(\Delta_h(f)) = \Delta_h \circ \Delta_h(f)$, which we further abbreviate to $\Delta_h^2(f)$ or, omitting the brackets entirely, to $\Delta_h^2 f$. This notation can be extended in an obvious way to obtain the further differences, so that, denoting the image of the element x under the function

$\Delta_h^n f$ by $\Delta_h^n f(x)$, where $n \in Z^+$, our general difference table now takes the form

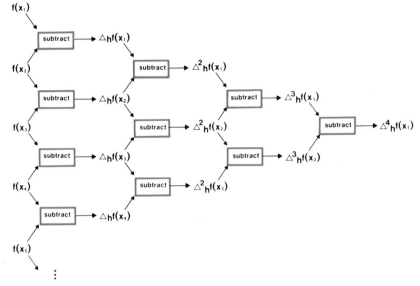

The quantities $\Delta_h^n f(x)$ are called *n*th differences (for any positive integer *n*). The operator Δ_h^n is called the *n*th difference operator for spacing *h*.

Definition 3
* * *
Definition 4
* * *

Exercise 2

If f_1, f_2 and f_3 are defined by

$$f_1 : x \longmapsto 2x \qquad (x \in R)$$

$$f_2 : x \longmapsto x^2 \qquad (x \in R)$$

$$f_3 : x \longmapsto 3x^3 + 2x \quad (x \in R)$$

find $\Delta_5^2(f_1)$, $\Delta_{0.7}^2(f_2)$, $\Delta_1^2(f_3)$. ∎

Exercise 2
(3 minutes)

Exercise 3

Complete each of the following statements by filling in the boxes : e.g. in (i)

$$\Delta_h(x \longmapsto \sin x) = \boxed{[x \longmapsto \sin(x+h) - \sin x]}$$

(All unspecified domains are *R* or *F* as appropriate.)

(i) $\Delta_h(x \longmapsto \sin x) = $ ☐

(ii) $\Delta_h \sin(x) = $ ☐

(iii) $\Delta_h \sin(2) = $ ☐

(iv) $\Delta_h^2(x \longmapsto \sin x) = $ ☐

(v) $\Delta_h^3(x \longmapsto x^3) = $ ☐ ∎

Exercise 3
(5 minutes)

25

Solution 1 Solution 1

$$\Delta_5(f_1) = [x \longmapsto f_1(x + 5) - f_1(x) \quad (x \in R)]$$

$$= [x \longmapsto 2(x + 5) - 2x \qquad (x \in R)]$$

$$= [x \longmapsto 10 \qquad (x \in R)]$$

$$\Delta_{0.7}(f_2) = [x \longmapsto 1.4x + 0.49 \qquad (x \in R)]$$

$$\Delta_{0.01}(f_3) = [x \longmapsto 0 \qquad (x \in R)] \qquad \blacksquare$$

Solution 2 Solution 2

From the solution of Exercise 1 we have

$$\Delta_5(f_1) = [x \longmapsto 10 \qquad (x \in R)]$$

Hence

$$\Delta_5^2(f_1) = \Delta_5(\Delta_5 f_1)$$

$$= [x \longmapsto 10 - 10 \qquad (x \in R)]$$

$$= [x \longmapsto 0 \qquad (x \in R)]$$

We also have from there

$$\Delta_{0.7}(f_2) = [x \longmapsto 1.4x + 0.49 \quad (x \in R)]$$

Hence

$$\Delta_{0.7}^2(f_2) = [x \longmapsto \{1.4(x + 0.7) + 0.49\}$$

$$- \{1.4x + 0.49\} \qquad (x \in R)]$$

$$= [x \longmapsto 0.98 \qquad (x \in R)]$$

Finally

$$\Delta_1(f_3) = [x \longmapsto \{3(x + 1)^3 + 2(x + 1)\}$$

$$- \{3x^3 + 2x\} \qquad (x \in R)]$$

$$= [x \longmapsto \{3x^3 + 9x^2 + 9x + 3 + 2x + 2\}$$

$$- \{3x^3 + 2x\} \qquad (x \in R)]$$

$$= [x \longmapsto 9x^2 + 9x + 5 \quad (x \in R)]$$

and

$$\Delta_1^2(f_3) = [x \longmapsto \{9(x + 1)^2 + 9(x + 1) + 5\}$$

$$- \{9x^2 + 9x + 5\} \quad (x \in R)]$$

$$= [x \longmapsto 18x + 18 \qquad (x \in R)] \qquad \blacksquare$$

Solution 3 Solution 3

(ii) $\sin(x + h) - \sin x$

(iii) $\sin(2 + h) - \sin 2$

(iv) $\Delta_h^2(x \longmapsto \sin x) = \Delta_h(x \longmapsto \sin(x + h) - \sin x)$

$$= [x \longmapsto \sin(x + 2h) - \sin(x + h)]$$

$$- [x \longmapsto \sin(x + h) - \sin x]$$

$$= [x \longmapsto \sin(x + 2h) - 2\sin(x + h) + \sin x]$$

(v) $\Delta_h^3(x \longmapsto x^3) = \Delta_h^2(x \longmapsto (x + h)^3 - x^3)$

$$= \Delta_h^2(x \longmapsto 3x^2 h + 3xh^2 + h^3)$$

$$= \Delta_h(x \longmapsto \{3h(x + h)^2 + 3h^2(x + h) + h^3\}$$

$$- \{3x^2 h + 3xh^2 + h^3\})$$

$$= \Delta_h(x \longmapsto 6h^2 x + 6h^3)$$

$$= [x \longmapsto \{6h^2(x + h) + 6h^3\} - \{6h^2 x + 6h^3\}]$$

$$= [x \longmapsto 6h^3] \qquad \blacksquare$$

You may find the following two exercises quite difficult. If so, try to understand the hints and solutions. *Do not spend too long on them* but, in any case, note the result of part (i) of the first exercise in the form given at the end of the solution.

Exercise 4

Exercise 4
(10 minutes)

(i) Is Δ_h compatible with addition on F? If your answer is YES, then see if you can recognize the induced binary operation in the image set.
(ii) Is Δ_h compatible with multiplication of F? If your answer is YES, then see if you can recognize the induced binary operation in the image set.

(For the definitions of compatibility and induced binary operation see *Unit 3, Operations and Morphisms*.) Some hints relating to this exercise are given below. ∎

Exercise 5

Exercise 5
(10 minutes)

If f and $g \in F$ are such that $\Delta_h(f) = \Delta_h(g)$, show that

$$f = g + p$$

where p is a periodic function with period h.* What more can you say about p if $\Delta_h(f) = \Delta_h(g)$ for all $h \in R$? ∎

Hints for the solution of Exercise 4

Hints

In order to get to grips with a problem of this type which requires a very general result, it is helpful to consider some simple special cases (*Polya*† pages 190–199).

For example, the following two functions

$$f_1 : x \longmapsto x^2 \qquad (x \in R)$$

and

$$f_2 : x \longmapsto x^2 + 1 \qquad (x \in R)$$

have the same image:

$$\Delta_h(f_1) : x \longmapsto 2hx + h^2 \quad (x \in R)$$

and

$$\Delta_h(f_2) : x \longmapsto 2hx + h^2 \quad (x \in R)$$

as you can easily check.

Also

$$g_1 : x \longmapsto x \qquad (x \in R)$$

and

$$g_2 : x \longmapsto x + 2 \qquad (x \in R)$$

have the same image:

$$\Delta_h(g_1) : x \longmapsto h \qquad (x \in R)$$

and

$$\Delta_h(g_2) : x \longmapsto h \qquad (x \in R)$$

So, instead of considering compatibility in general, let us first see if it works for these special cases: e.g.

$$\text{is } \Delta_h(f_1 + g_1) = \Delta_h(f_2 + g_2)?$$

and

$$\text{is } \Delta_h(f_1 \times g_1) = \Delta_h(f_2 \times g_2)?$$

When you have answered these questions you should be able to answer at least one of (i) and (ii).

* A function f with domain R is said to be a periodic function with period h if $f(x + h) = f(x)$, for all $x \in R$. The graph of such a function "repeats" itself at intervals of length h. E.g. the sine function is periodic with period 2π.

Definition 5
*

† G. Polya, *How to Solve it*, Open University ed. (Doubleday Anchor Books 1970). This book is the set book for the Mathematics Foundation Course; it is referred to in the text as *Polya*.

Solution 4   **Solution 4**

We use the notation introduced in the hints and deal with case (ii) first.

$$\Delta_h(f_1 \times g_1) = \Delta_h(x \longmapsto x^3)$$

$$= [x \longmapsto (x + h)^3 - x^3]$$

$$\Delta_h(f_2 \times g_2) = \Delta_h(x \longmapsto x^3 + 2x^2 + x + 2)$$

$$= [x \longmapsto \{(x + h)^3 + 2(x + h)^2 + (x + h) + 2\}$$

$$- \{x^3 + 2x^2 + x + 2\}]$$

and we can easily see that $\Delta_h(f_1 \times g_1) \neq \Delta_h(f_2 \times g_2)$. So this one example shows that Δ_h is not compatible with multiplication on F.

The above illustrates an important point: whenever we wish to decide whether a general statement about the elements of a set is true or false, then if we can find *any* elements of the set for which the statement is false, then it is false. On the other hand, if we find one element of the set for which the statement is true, this does *not* prove that it is true for all elements of the set. In this case, our general statement is

"Δ_h is compatible with multiplication on F"

and this is a statement about all the elements of F. We have found four elements f_1, f_2, g_1, g_2, for which the statement is false; therefore it is false.

On the other hand, as you probably found if you followed through our hint, the statement

"Δ_h is compatible with addition on F"

is true for f_1, f_2, g_1, g_2. So we have not yet reached a conclusion on (i). We can now either continue our search for elements F for which the statement is false, or try to *prove* that it is true, whatever elements of F we choose. The course we adopt depends on our *intuition*. Do we feel that it is true, or do we feel that it is false? If our intuition is not yet sufficiently developed in this problem to influence our feelings we should try more examples.

Finally, in this case, we will have to sit down and prove that the statement is true, as follows:

Let $f_1, f_2, g_1, g_2 \in F$ and be such that

$$\Delta_h(f_1) = \Delta_h(f_2)$$ Equation (1)

$$\Delta_h(g_1) = \Delta_h(g_2)$$ Equation (2)

Then

$$\Delta_h(f_1 + g_1) = \Delta_h(x \longmapsto f_1(x) + g_1(x))$$

$$= [x \longmapsto \{f_1(x + h) + g_1(x + h)\}$$

$$- \{f_1(x) + g_1(x)\}]$$

$$= [x \longmapsto f_1(x + h) - f_1(x)]$$

$$+ [x \longmapsto g_1(x + h) - g_1(x)]$$

$$= \Delta_h(f_1) + \Delta_h(g_1)$$

Similarly $\Delta_h(f_2 + g_2) = \Delta_h(f_2) + \Delta_h(g_2)$. It follows from Equations (1) and (2) that

$$\Delta_h(f_1 + g_1) = \Delta_h(f_2 + g_2)$$

and since f_1, f_2, g_1, g_2 are any elements of F, that Δ_h is *compatible with addition on F*. The induced binary operation $\square$ on the image set is defined by

$$\Delta_h(f) \;\square\; \Delta_h(g) = \Delta_h(f + g) \quad \text{for all } f, g \in F$$

and from our working above we recognize $\square$ as the addition of functions, i.e.

$$\boxed{\Delta_h(f + g) = \Delta_h(f) + \Delta_h(g)}$$

∎

Solution 5

Since

$$\Delta_h(f) = \Delta_h(g)$$
$$\Delta_h(f) - \Delta_h(g) = O$$

where O here stands for the constant function

$$x \longmapsto 0 \quad (x \in R)$$

For a real function g, we define $-g$ by

$$-g : x \longmapsto -g(x)$$

where $-g$ has the same domain as g. Then we can write

$$\Delta_h(f) - \Delta_h(g) = \Delta_h(f) + (-\Delta_h(g)) = \Delta_h(f) + \Delta_h(-g)$$

and by the result of Exercise 4 we have

$$\Delta_h(f + (-g)) = O \quad \text{or} \quad \Delta_h(f - g) = O$$

Now, if we put $p = f - g$, then $\Delta_h(p) = O$, so we have

$$p(x + h) - p(x) = 0$$

Equation (3)

for all $x \in R$, so that p is periodic with period h, from which the required result now follows, viz. $f = g + p$.

If Equation (3) is also true for all $h \in R$, then, putting $x = 0$, we have

$$p(h) - p(0) = 0$$

and so

$$p(h) = p(0)$$

for all $h \in R$, i.e. p is a constant function, whose one image is $p(0)$. (For the definition of a constant function see *Unit 1, Functions*.) ∎

4.2.2 Differences of Polynomials

When you extrapolated the *Highway Code* table of stopping distances discussed in Section 4.1.3 to 70 miles per hour, you used the fact that the second differences of this table were all the same. When you found 37^2 by extrapolating a table of squares that stopped at 36^2, you again used the fact that the second differences were all the same. Perhaps you wondered whether there were any other functions for which the second differences were all the same, or whether the differences for a table of cubes would have any similar property.

Following our argument similar to that of Exercise 4.2.1.5, we could investigate real functions, f, for which $\Delta_h^2 f$ is a constant function *for all* $h \in R$, and try to deduce what the f looks like. This would certainly be a satisfactory approach, but it could prove quite difficult. So we have chosen the somewhat easier, but less satisfactory approach of asking you to verify the result given in the following exercise.

Exercise 1

Verify that for the function

$$f : x \longmapsto ax^2 + bx + c \quad (x \in R)$$

(i) $\Delta_h f$ is a linear function,
(ii) $\Delta_h^2 f$ is a constant function. ∎

From this last exercise it follows that a general function with the required property that its second differences are all the same is

$$x \longmapsto ax^2 + bx + c \quad (x \in R)$$

It does not, however, follow that this is the only type of function whose second differences are constant (whatever h), although this is in fact true. Any expression of the form $ax^2 + bx + c$ (with $a \neq 0$) is called a quadratic polynomial in x, and a function that maps x to a quadratic polynomial in x is a called a quadratic function.

Exercise 2

The graph of a quadratic function is a parabola. If you are not familiar with this curve you may like to choose numerical values for a, b, c and sketch one such curve. ∎

The problem we solved can be generalized: can we find a general (real) function with constant third differences, or indeed with constant mth differences where m is any positive integer? Try to guess the answer before proceeding. A plausible guess for a general function with constant third differences is

$$f : x \longmapsto ax^3 + bx^2 + cx + d \quad (x \in R)$$

where a, b, c, d are any real numbers. Any expression of the form $ax^3 + bx^2 + cx + d$ (with $a \neq 0$) is called a cubic polynomial in x, and the function f is a cubic function. Taking the first differences of f we have

$$\Delta_h f(x) = \{a(x + h)^3 + b(x + h)^2 + c(x + h) + d\}$$
$$- \{ax^3 + bx^2 + cx + d\}$$
$$= 3ahx^2 + (3ah^2 + 2bh)x + (ah^3 + bh^2 + ch)$$

The important thing to notice is that the right-hand side is a quadratic polynomial in x; that is, we have shown that

$$\Delta_h \text{ (cubic function)} = \text{(quadratic function)}$$

Since we already know, by Exercise 1, that

$$\Delta_h \text{ (quadratic function)} = \text{(linear function)}$$

and

$$\Delta_h \text{ (linear function)} = \text{(constant function)}$$

it follows that any cubic function has constant third differences.

This argument can be generalized. The most general (real) function of the same type as a cubic or quadratic function is

$$f : x \longmapsto a_n x^n + a_{n-1} x^{n-1} + \cdots + a_1 x + a_0 \quad (x \in R)$$

where n is any positive integer or 0, and $a_n, a_{n-1}, \ldots, a_1, a_0$ are any real numbers, called the coefficients.

Provided that $a_n \neq 0$, the expression $a_n x^n + \cdots + a_0$ is called a polynomial of degree n and the corresponding function a polynomial function of degree n. You can complete the argument for yourself.

Definition 5
* *
Definition 6
* * *
Definition 7
* * *

Exercise 3

Which of the following are polynomials?

(i) $x^4 - 6x + 1$,   (ii) $(x - 3)(x + 2)$,

(iii) $\dfrac{x + 5}{x - 3}$,   (iv) $2x + 4$,   (v) 7.

Once again, if you find the following exercise difficult (or if you are short of time) try to understand the solution. In any case you should note the result of the exercise. ■

Exercise 3
(2 minutes)

Exercise 4

If f is a polynomial function of degree n, is $\Delta_h f$ a polynomial function and, if so, what is its degree? What do you conclude about the difference table of a polynomial function, and, in particular, about the nth difference of a polynomial function of degree n? ■

Exercise 4
(2 minutes)

Solution 1

Solution 1

(i) $\Delta_h f = [x \longmapsto \{a(x + h)^2 + b(x + h) + c\}$

$$- \{ax^2 + bx + c\} \qquad (x \in R)]$$

$$= [x \longmapsto 2ahx + ah^2 + bh \quad (x \in R)]$$

which is linear.

(ii) $\Delta_h^2 f = [x \longmapsto \{2ah(x + h) + ah^2 + bh\}$

$$- \{2ahx + ah^2 + bh\} \qquad (x \in R)]$$

$$= [x \longmapsto 2ah^2 \qquad (x \in R)]$$

which is constant. ∎

Solution 2

Solution 2

With $b = c = 0$, specimen curves are

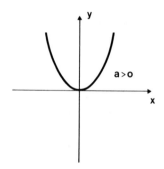

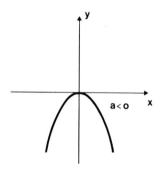

For any other choice of a, b and c, a similar curve is obtained, displaced
from the origin. ∎

Solution 3

Solution 3

  (i) *is* a polynomial (quartic).
 (ii) *is* a polynomial (quadratic).
(iii) is *not* a polynomial.
 (iv) *is* a polynomial (linear).
  (v) *is* a polynomial (constant). ∎

Solution 4

$$f : x \longmapsto a_n x^n + a_{n-1} x^{n-1} + \cdots + a_1 x + a_0 \quad (x \in R)$$

$$\Delta_h f : x \longmapsto \{a_n(x+h)^n + a_{n-1}(x+h)^{n-1} + \cdots + a_1(x+h) + a_0\}$$

$$- \{a_n x^n + a_{n-1} x^{n-1} + \cdots + a_1 x + a_0\} \quad (x \in R)$$

We now expand each of the brackets $(x + h)^k$, $k = 2, 3, \ldots, n$, using the binomial expansion, e.g.

$$(x + h)^n = x^n + \binom{n}{1} x^{n-1} h + \binom{n}{2} x^{n-2} h^2 + \cdots + h^n$$

Thus $\{a_n(x+h)^n - a_n x^n\}$ is

$$\{a_n(x^n + nx^{n-1}h + \cdots + h^n) - a_n x^n\}$$

$$= a_n(nx^{n-1}h + \cdots + h^n)$$

$$= \text{polynomial of degree } (n-1)$$

We can similarly expand each of the terms, and then collect all the results. But the essential thing to notice here is that we start with f, a polynomial function of degree n, and we recognize $\Delta_h f$ to be another polynomial function, but the highest power of the variable x is now $(n-1)$, i.e. $\Delta_h f$ *is a polynomial function of degree* $(n-1)$.

Thus Δ_h (nth degree function) = (function of degree $n-1$).

Similarly

$$\Delta_h^2 \text{ (} n \text{th degree function)}$$

$$= \Delta_h \text{ (function of degree } n-1)$$

$$= \text{(function of degree } n-2)$$

and

$$\Delta_h^n \text{ (} n \text{th degree function)}$$

$$= \text{(function of degree } n-n)$$

$$= \text{(constant function)} \qquad \blacksquare$$

4.2.3 Summary

In this section we examined the behaviour of successive columns of the difference table for a tabulated function, and showed how they could be regarded as being generated by successive applications of the difference operator Δ_h, to the original function. This operator provides a convenient notation for expressing formulas involving differences succinctly. It will be shown in a later unit that it has affinities with the differentiation operator. Δ_h is compatible with the operation of addition (and subtraction), which is an important and useful result.

We then went on to show that the nth differences of a polynomial function of degree n are all equal. Conversely, if we find that the nth differences in a difference table are all equal (whatever h), we may assume that the function generating the table is a polynomial of degree n.

4.3 NON-LINEAR INTERPOLATION

4.3.0 Introduction

In one of the exercises you did earlier in this unit (Exercise 4.1.2.3) you saw that linear interpolation tended to be more accurate the smaller the spacing of the tabular points. The designers of good tables of commonly-used functions, such as the logarithm and trigonometric functions, take care that the tabular spacing is small enough to make linear interpolation accurate and convenient. For a table that will not see so much use, however, the designer may well choose to economize by computing the value of the function for relatively few tabular points; he is particularly likely to do this if each tabular value demands a lot of computing effort and if the resulting table will be used only once because it arises from a unique situation, as in the case of the function mentioned in the introduction to this unit, which describes the lifting effect of the air on particular parts of an aeroplane wing under particular flying conditions. In such cases the tabular spacing is likely to be too large to justify linear interpolation and more sophisticated methods are necessary.

The purpose of this part of the unit is to show you one such method, in which the tabulated function is approximated between the tabular points not by a linear function but by a polynomial function. You may ask: "What is special about polynomial functions; why not use some other function such as the sine or cosine?" One reason is simply that polynomial interpolation is very convenient, largely because of the nice properties of the differences of polynomials which you studied in the previous section; and convenience is a very important factor in making a choice of numerical methods.

A further reason for using polynomials is contained in a theorem proved by a German mathematician, Weierstrass, who lived in the last century. This theorem (whose proof we shall not consider here) states that any continuous* function can be approximated over any desired interval to any desired accuracy by means of some polynomial. Unfortunately Weierstrass' theorem has the annoying feature of so many so-called *existence theorems* in mathematics: it tells us that the polynomial exists, but not how to find it. In the rest of this section we shall not use Weierstrass' theorem except to give confidence in the ultimate validity of polynomial approximation methods, and concentrate instead on practical methods for finding approximating polynomials and for interpolating with their help.

Karl W. T. Weierstrass (1815–1897)

---

* The term *continuous* in this context means that the graph of the function is continuous: i.e. there are no breaks or jumps in the curve. The concept will be studied more thoroughly in *Unit 7, Sequences and Limits I*.

4.3.1 Fitting a Linear Function

The very simplest type of polynomial interpolation is the same thing as linear interpolation, which we have already considered in Section 4.1.2; for the linear functions used there to approximate the tabulated functions are, by the definition of "polynomial function" given in Section 4.2.2, none other than polynomial functions of degree 1. Before discussing non-linear interpolation, therefore, we recapitulate the principles of linear interpolation using a slightly different viewpoint from the one used in the section devoted to this topic.

In linear interpolation we approximate the function between two successive tabular points, say x_k and x_{k+1}, by a linear function that fits (i.e. has the same tabular values as) the tabulated function at those two tabular points. (See figure.)

This linear function may be denoted by l, where

$$l : x \longmapsto ax + b \qquad (x \in [x_k, x_{k+1}])$$

and a and b are two real numbers.

Exercise 1

Why did we use $[x_k, x_{k+1}]$, rather than R, for the domain of l? ◾

We have stipulated that l must fit the tabulated function at x_k and x_{k+1}; that is,

$$\left. \begin{array}{l} l(x_k) = f(x_k) \\ l(x_{k+1}) = f(x_{k+1}) \end{array} \right\}$$

These two conditions are just enough to determine the two constants a and b in the definition of l; for, they are equivalent to

$$\left. \begin{array}{l} x_k a + b = f(x_k) \\ x_{k+1} a + b = f(x_{k+1}) \end{array} \right\}$$

and since the tabular points x_k, x_{k+1} and the values $f(x_k)$, $f(x_{k+1})$ are known, we can treat these equations as a pair of simultaneous equations for the two unknowns a and b.

Exercise 2

Solve the equations for a and b and hence obtain an explicit formula for $l(x)$ in terms of x and tabular points and values.

(The solution of this exercise requires a certain degree of facility with algebraic manipulation. If you do not have this facility, read the solution and then work through the details yourself step by step, if you have the time. The important thing is to take note of the result in Equation (3). In general, throughout this section, the technical details (some of which are omitted, in any case) are not as important as your understanding of what we are trying to do and an appreciation of the results.) ◾

Solution 1

Solution 1

The graph of *l* is to be a segment of a straight line : not a complete straight line. The algebraic equivalent of this geometric condition is the restriction on the domain of *l*. Evidently, we wish to approximate to the complete curve like this:

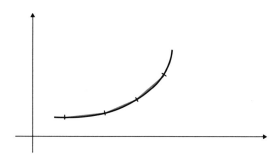

not like this:

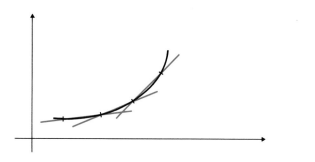

∎

Solution 2

Solution 2

The solution of the simultaneous equations is

$$a = \frac{f(x_{k+1}) - f(x_k)}{x_{k+1} - x_k}$$

$$b = \frac{x_{k+1} f(x_k) - x_k f(x_{k+1})}{x_{k+1} - x_k}$$

which when substituted into the formula for *l(x)* gives

$$l(x) = \frac{x_{k+1} - x}{x_{k+1} - x_k} f(x_k) + \frac{x - x_k}{x_{k+1} - x_k} f(x_{k+1})$$

Equation (1)

We shall carry this solution a little further and eliminate *x* in favour of the variable

$$\theta = \frac{x - x_k}{x_{k+1} - x_k}$$

which represents the proportion in which the number x divides the interval $[x_k, x_{k+1}]$ (see figure).

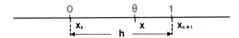

Noticing that

$$\frac{x_{k+1} - x}{x_{k+1} - x_k} = 1 - \frac{x - x_k}{x_{k+1} - x_k} = 1 - \theta$$

Equation (1) now becomes

$$l(x) = f(x_k) + \{f(x_{k+1}) - f(x_k)\}\theta, \quad (x \in [x_k, x_{k+1}]) \hspace{3cm} \text{Equation (2)}$$

A neater way to write Equation (2) is to use the difference operator defined in Section 4.2.1; it then simplifies to

$$l(x) = f(x_k) + \theta \cdot \Delta_h f(x_k) \quad (x \in [x_k, x_{k+1}]) \hspace{2cm} \blacksquare \hspace{1cm} \text{Equation (3)}$$

Exercise 3

Exercise 3
(3 minutes)

Use Equation (3) to estimate $\tan(1.444)$ from the table at the right, and compare with the true value (to three decimal places), $\tan(1.444) = 7.844$.

x	$\tan x$
1.43	7.055
1.44	7.602
1.45	8.238
1.46	8.989

(You could, of course, answer this exercise by the methods of Section 4.1.2, but in order to get a feeling for our present methods, we suggest you do it using Equation (3).) $\blacksquare$

Solution 3

The difference table is shown at the right. The interval $[x_k, x_{k+1}]$ containing 1.444 is $[1.44, 1.45]$; hence $x_k = 1.44$ and

$$\theta = \frac{0.004}{0.01} = \frac{4}{10}$$

x	$\tan x$	$\Delta_{0.01}(\tan x)$
1.43	7.055	
		0.547
1.44	7.602	
		0.636
1.45	8.238	
		0.751
1.46	8.989	

Equation (3) thus gives

$$\tan(1.444) \simeq 7.602 + \tfrac{4}{10} \times 0.636 = 7.856$$

which is the estimate for $\tan(1.444)$ given by linear interpolation. The error of 0.012 shows that the approximation of $\tan x$ by $l(x)$ does not give good accuracy in this range. ∎

4.3.2 Polynomial Interpolation

When linear interpolation is not very accurate, as in the preceding example, it indicates that the tabulated function is not very accurately represented by the linear function $l(x)$ over the interval $[x_k, x_{k+1}]$. In such cases we can try to allow for the non-linearity by using a simple non-linear approximating function instead of a linear one. If the approximating function is to be a polynomial, then the simplest (i.e. of lowest degree) non-linear possibility is the quadratic function

$$q: x \longmapsto ax^2 + bx + c$$

To complete the specification of this function we need values for the three constants a, b, c, and also a specification of the domain. Following the method used in the preceding section we could try to determine a, b, and c by requiring that q must fit the tabulated function at two successive tabular points, say x_k and x_{k+1}. Can you see the difficulty that would arise? We would get two simultaneous equations

$$\left. \begin{array}{l} x_k^2 a + x_k b + c = f(x_k) \\ x_{k+1}^2 a + x_{k+1} b + c = f(x_{k+1}) \end{array} \right\}$$

but they would not be enough to determine a, b, and c (see figure).

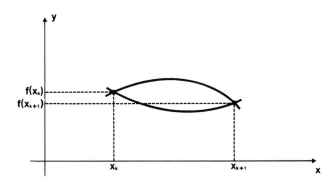

To find three unknown quantities we need *three* simultaneous equations. There are various ways of obtaining a third equation; the simplest, and the only one we shall consider here, is to require that q shall fit the tabulated function at *three* consecutive tabular points instead of just two (see figure).

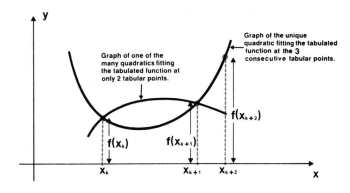

Graph of one of the many quadratics fitting the tabulated function at only 2 tabular points.

Graph of the unique quadratic fitting the tabulated function at the 3 consecutive tabular points.

Calling these three points x_k, x_{k+1}, x_{k+2}, we then have the three equations

$$\left. \begin{array}{l} q(x_k) = x_k^2 a + x_k b + c = f(x_k) \\ q(x_{k+1}) = x_{k+1}^2 a + x_{k+1} b + c = f(x_{k+1}) \\ q(x_{k+2}) = x_{k+2}^2 a + x_{k+2} b + c = f(x_{k+2}) \end{array} \right\}$$

Equations (1)

and since the number of equations is now equal to the number of unknowns, the equations now contain enough information to determine a, b, and c.

It remains to specify the domain of $q(x)$. Because of Equations (1) the domain must include at least the numbers x_k, x_{k+1}, and x_{k+2}, and, if the function is to be useful for interpolation, it must also include intermediate values; thus the least domain for $q(x)$ is $[x_k, x_{k+2}]$. The graph of this function

$$q: x \longmapsto ax^2 + bx + c \quad (x \in [x_k, x_{k+2}])$$

is the one shown in the last figure. Of course, if the function were required (and were suitable) for extrapolation, the domain could easily be extended.

To find the three constants a, b, c, the obvious method of proceeding is to solve the three simultaneous equations (1).

There are standard techniques for solving such a system of equations; you will meet some of them in one of the units on *Linear Algebra*. Here, however, we are not concerned with the techniques but only with the final result, which can be put in the form

$$
\begin{aligned}
q(x) &= ax^2 + bx + c \\
&= \frac{(x - x_{k+1})(x - x_{k+2})}{(x_k - x_{k+1})(x_k - x_{k+2})} f(x_k) \\
&\quad + \frac{(x - x_k)(x - x_{k+2})}{(x_{k+1} - x_k)(x_{k+1} - x_{k+2})} f(x_{k+1}) \\
&\quad + \frac{(x - x_k)(x - x_{k+1})}{(x_{k+2} - x_k)(x_{k+2} - x_{k+1})} f(x_{k+2})
\end{aligned}
$$

Joseph-Louis Lagrange (1736–1813)

Equation (2)

The expression on the right is called Lagrange's interpolation polynomial; it is the analogue of Equation (1) of 4.3.1 for the linear case. (There is no point in your learning this formula by heart.)

Definition 1
* *

Just as in our treatment of the linear case we can simplify Equation (2) by using the variable θ, related to x as in the figure:

<!-- number line figure: 0, θ, 1, 2 marked; x_k, x, x_{k+1}, x_{k+2}; intervals h, h -->

Then Equation (2) becomes (after some technical details, which are omitted) a quadratic polynomial in θ:

$$
\begin{aligned}
q(x) &= \tfrac{1}{2}\theta^2 \{f(x_{k+2}) - 2f(x_{k+1}) + f(x_k)\} \\
&\quad + \theta \{-\tfrac{1}{2}f(x_{k+2}) + 2f(x_{k+1}) - \tfrac{3}{2}f(x_k)\} + f(x_k)
\end{aligned}
$$

Equation (3)

This formula is not very important in itself; it is only written down so that you can see whether you recognize the coefficient of θ^2 (i.e. the number multiplying θ^2 in the first term on the right). Apart from the factor $\tfrac{1}{2}$ this coefficient is $\Delta_h^2 f(x_k)$. The coefficient of θ looks a little more complicated but it can still be written in the terms of the difference operator; it is $\Delta_h f(x_k) - \tfrac{1}{2}\Delta_h^2 f(x_k)$. Using these expressions for the coefficients we can write Equation (3) in the very concise form

$$q(x) = f(x_k) + \theta \Delta_h f(x_k) + \tfrac{1}{2}\theta(\theta - 1)\Delta_h^2 f(x_k) \quad (x \in [x_k, x_{k+2}])$$

Equation (4)

This is a special case of a general formula called the Gregory-Newton Formula.

Definition 2
* * *

Example 1

Example 1

As our illustration of how the Gregory-Newton formula is used, let us again consider the *Highway Code* table, i.e.

Speed (mile/h)	Stopping Distance (ft)	First Differences	Second Differences
20	40		
30	75	35	10
40	120	45	10
50	175	55	10
60	240	65	

We are interested in estimating the stopping distance in feet when travelling at 24 mile/h.

In this case we would choose $x_k = 20$ and $x_{k+1} = 30$. Then

$$\theta = \frac{x - x_k}{x_{k+1} - x_k} = \frac{24 - 20}{30 - 20} = \frac{4}{10}$$

and we have $h = 10$; Equation (4) becomes

$$q(24) = f(20) + \frac{4}{10} \times \Delta_{10} f(20) + \frac{1}{2} \times \frac{4}{10} \times \left(-\frac{6}{10}\right) \Delta_{10}^2 f(20)$$

$$= 40 + \frac{140}{10} - \frac{120}{100}$$

$$= 40 + 14 - 1.2 = 52.8 \text{ ft} \qquad \blacksquare$$

Exercise 1

Exercise 1
(5 minutes)

Use the Gregory-Newton quadratic interpolation formula to calculate tan (1.444) from the table at the right, and compare with the result obtained by linear interpolation in Exercise 4.3.1.3, and with the correct result 7.844.

x	$\tan x$
1.43	7.055
1.44	7.602
1.45	8.238
1.46	8.989

$\blacksquare$

Solution 1

The difference table is shown at the right. The number 1.444 lies in the interval $[x_k, x_{k+2}]$ with $x_k = 1.43$ or 1.44: either value for x_k may be used.

x	$\tan x$	Δ	Δ^2
1.43	7.055		
		547	
1.44	7.602		89
		636	
1.45	8.238		115
		751	
1.46	8.989		

$x_k = 1.43$

$\theta = 1.4$

$q(x) = 7.055 + 1.4 \times 0.547$

$\qquad + \dfrac{1.4 \times 0.4}{2} \times 0.089$

$\qquad = 7.055 + 0.766 + 0.025$

$\qquad = 7.846$

$x_k = 1.44$

$\theta = 0.4$

$q(x) = \underbrace{7.602 + 0.4 \times 0.636}_{\text{linear interpolation}}$

$\qquad + \dfrac{0.4 \times (-0.6)}{2} \times 0.115$

$\qquad = 7.602 + 0.254 + (-0.012)$

$\qquad = 7.844$ ∎

Choosing $x_k = 1.43$, our solution agrees within 0.002 with the correct value. When x_k is chosen to be 1.44, the agreement is exact to 3 decimal places. Using linear interpolation (see p. 38), we found $\tan(1.444) = 7.856$, which is not very accurate.

The general Gregory-Newton formula for nth degree polynomial interpolation to the function f is

$$g(x) = f(x_k) + \theta\Delta_h f(x_k) + \tfrac{1}{2}\theta(\theta - 1)\Delta_h^2 f(x_k) + \cdots$$

$$+ \frac{1}{n!}\theta(\theta - 1)(\theta - 2)\cdots(\theta - n + 1)\Delta_h^n f(x_k)$$

Definition 3
* * *

The domain over which it is useful for interpolation is the interval $[x_k, x_{k+n}]$. It is the basic formula for polynomial interpolation (although not the most practical when the degree of the polynomial is higher than 2).

4.3.3 Formulas from Tables

Although the principal application of the Gregory-Newton formula is to non-linear interpolation, it can also be used for what is essentially non-linear extrapolation of polynomial functions. If the purpose of an extrapolation is merely to find the next member of a sequence of numbers such as $1, 3, 5, 7, \ldots$ or $40, 75, 120, 175, 240, \ldots$ (the *Highway Code* stopping distances, considered earlier in this unit), then there is no need for the Gregory-Newton formula; we simply build up the function directly from the difference table as explained in Section 4.1.3. The Gregory-Newton formula does come in useful, however, when we want a formula that will give *all* the non-tabulated elements of the sequence. For example, we can use the Gregory-Newton formula to obtain a general formula giving the nth element of the sequence whose first five elements are

$$1^2, 1^2 + 2^2, 1^2 + 2^2 + 3^3, 1^2 + 2^2 + 3^2 + 4^2, 1^2 + 2^2 + 3^2$$
$$+ 4^2 + 5^2, \ldots$$

— that is, it gives us a formula for the sum of the squares of the first n natural numbers. Such formulas for sums of powers will be used in *Unit 9, Integration I* for calculating areas. A typical case to which the results are applied is illustrated in the figure; the area between the curve and the x-axis is approximately a set of rectangles.

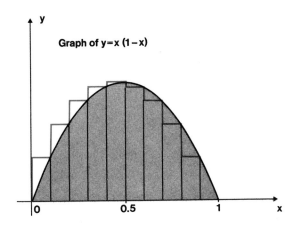

Graph of y=x (1−x)

The width of each rectangle is $\frac{1}{10}$; the height of the nth rectangle from the left is $\frac{n}{10}\left(1 - \frac{n}{10}\right)$, so that its area is $\frac{n}{100} - \frac{n^2}{1000}$. The sum of the areas of the 10 rectangles can be evaluated using formulas derived in this section. (For further details see *Unit 9, Integration I*.)

To work out the method, we consider once again the *Highway Code* table of stopping distances.

s Speed (mile/h)	d Stopping Distance (ft)	Differences	
		First	Second
20	40		
30	75	35	10
40	120	45	10
50	175	55	10
60	240	65	

Can we deduce from the table a polynomial formula that gives the stopping distance, d, directly in terms of the speed, s? That is, can we find a polynomial function p such that

$$d = p(s)$$

holds for all the tabular points?

The first differences are not constant; therefore p is not of degree 1. On the other hand, the tabulated second differences *are* constant, so that the tabular values can be fitted by a polynomial of degree 2, i.e. a quadratic.

The table does not *prove* that the degree of the polynomial is 2, nor even that the function $s \longmapsto d$ is a polynomial at all. But a quadratic polynomial fitting all the tabulated points does exist, and the table does come from a physical law, so that it is good scientific method to adopt the quadratic as a working hypothesis until some positive reason for rejecting it turns up (such a reason would exist, for example, if one were foolish enough to try to extrapolate to supersonic speeds or even to speeds of 150 mile/h). See also the discussion in Section 4.1.1.

One way of finding the polynomial function p would be to substitute three different tabulated values of s into the formula

$$d = p(s) = as^2 + bs + c$$

together with the corresponding values of d, and solve the three resulting simultaneous equations for a, b, c. It is much quicker, however, to use the result of Section 4.3.2, where a general problem of this type was solved and gave us the Gregory-Newton formula (4) of 4.3.2. In the present notation this formula is

$$d(s) = d(s_k) + \theta \Delta_{10}\, d(s_k) + \frac{\theta(\theta - 1)}{2} \Delta_{10}^2\, d(s_k) \quad (s \in [s_k, s_{k+2}]) \qquad \text{Equation (1)}$$

where θ is defined by

$$\theta = \frac{s - s_k}{s_{k+1} - s_k}$$

It does not matter which tabular point we call s_k as long as we know $d(s_k)$, $\Delta_{10}\, d(s_k)$ and $\Delta_{10}^2\, d(s_k)$. Let us take $s_k = 20$. With this and the data from the table Equation (1) becomes

$$d = 40 + 35\theta + 10\frac{\theta(\theta - 1)}{2} \quad (s \in [20, 40])$$

$$= 40 + 30\theta + 5\theta^2 \qquad \text{Equation (2)}$$

with

$$\theta = \frac{s - 20}{10} \qquad \text{Equation (3)}$$

Substituting θ from Equation (3) into Equation (2) we have

$$d = 40 + 30\frac{s - 20}{10} + 5\frac{(s - 20)^2}{10^2}$$

$$= 40 + 3s - 60 + \frac{s^2}{20} - 2s + 20$$

$$= s + \frac{s^2}{20} \quad (s \in [20, 40]) \qquad \text{Equation (4)}$$

The polynomial function $s \longmapsto d$ defined by Equation (4) has been chosen to fit the tabular values over the interval [20, 40], and since only one quadratic will fit three tabular points, it is the unique quadratic function that does so. Consequently, if we wish to fit the tabular values by a quadratic over the tabular range, or some greater range, we must again use the polynomial in Equation (4). This, then, is our extrapolation formula:

$$p(s) = s + \frac{s^2}{20}$$

Equation (5)

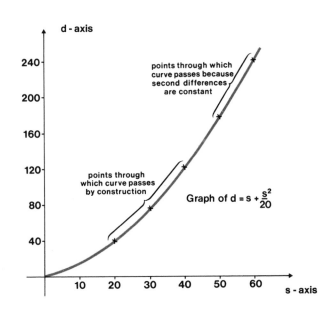

We know from the way it was calculated that the polynomial in Equation (5) fits the tabular values in the interval [20, 40], i.e. for $s = 20$, 30 and 40. We know from the constancy of the column of second differences that there is a quadratic to fit all the tabular values, and from the uniqueness of the Gregory-Newton formula that this quadratic must be the one in Equation (5), so that this polynomial fits the tabular values $s = 50$ and 60 as well. For values of s other than these five, the table does not tell us whether the polynomial in Equation (5) is an accurate formula for stopping distance; but, as explained earlier in this section, the formula is a good hypothesis for testing against whatever further information we may have about the source of the numbers in the table. As it happens, in the present case, the "further information" to some extent supports the hypothesis. If you look again at the *Highway Code* you will see that the stopping distances given are broken down into "thinking distances" and "braking distances" (see table below),

Speed	Distance		
	Stopping	Thinking	Braking
20	40	20	20
30	75	30	45
40	120	40	80
50	175	50	125
60	240	60	180

and these two distances correspond exactly to the two terms in the polynomial in Equation (5). As a last piece of detective work, you may like to work out for yourself just what physical assumptions one might adopt to justify the particular numbers used by the Ministry of Transport for the two components of stopping distance.

Let us now return to the problem mentioned earlier: finding a formula for the sum of the squares of the first n natural numbers. The method of solving it is almost identical with the one used in the *Highway Code* example, so you can probably do it for yourself with a little help.

Exercise 1

Writing $S_2(n)$ for the sum of the squares of the first n natural numbers, i.e. for $1^2 + 2^2 + \cdots + n^2$, tabulate the value of $S_2(n)$ for $n = 1, 2, 3, 4, 5, 6$. What is the lowest degree of a polynomial in n that will fit these values? ■

Exercise 2

Find the polynomial of lowest degree that fits $S_2(n)$ for the values tabulated in your previous solution. Check it by considering $S_2(7)$. (In the subsequent text we shall show that the formula for $S_2(n)$ is correct for every positive integral n.) ■

Exercise 3

Find

(i) the sum of the first n natural numbers and
(ii) the sum of the cubes of the first n natural numbers. ■

(If you are short of time, do not spend much time on this exercise: read and understand the solution, and note the results.)

Exercise 1
(3 minutes)

Exercise 2
(10 minutes)

Exercise 3
(10 minutes)

Solution 1

Solution 1

n	$S_2(n)$	Δ	Δ^2	Δ^3
1	1			
2	5	4		
3	14	9	5	
4	30	16	7	2
5	55	25	9	2
6	91	36	11	2

Since the column of third differences is the first that is constant, the polynomial is of at least the third degree. ■

Solution 2

Solution 2

Gregory-Newton formula with $x_k = 1$ becomes:

$$S_2(n) = 1 + 4\theta + 5\frac{\theta(\theta - 1)}{2} + 2\frac{\theta(\theta - 1)(\theta - 2)}{6}$$

with $\theta = n - 1$.

Simplifying gives:

$$S_2(n) = \frac{6 + 24(n - 1) + 15(n - 1)(n - 2) + 2(n - 1)(n - 2)(n - 3)}{6}$$

$$= \frac{6 + 24n - 24 + 15n^2 - 45n + 30 + 2n^3 - 12n^2 + 22n - 12}{6}$$

$$= \frac{n + 3n^2 + 2n^3}{6}$$

or

$$S_2(n) = \frac{n(n + 1)(2n + 1)}{6}$$

■

Solution 3

Solution 3

(i) $S_1(n) = 1 + 2 + 3 + \cdots + n$

The difference table for $S_1(n)$ is

n	$S_1(n)$	$\Delta_1 S_1(n)$	$\Delta_1^2 S_1(n)$
1	1		
2	3	2	
3	6	3	1
4	10	4	1
5	15	5	1
6	21	6	1

Since the second differences are constant, the polynomial is of second degree (at least).

The Newton-Gregory formula for the quadratic polynomial $S(n)$ is

$$S(n) = S(n_k) + \theta\Delta_1 S(n_k) + \tfrac{1}{2}\theta(\theta - 1)\Delta_1^2 S(n_k)$$

We take $n_k = 1$, and $\theta = \dfrac{n - n_k}{n_{k+1} - n_k} = \dfrac{n - 1}{2 - 1} = n - 1$

It follows that

$$S(n) = 1 + (n-1) \times 2 + \tfrac{1}{2}(n-1)(n-2) \times 1$$
$$= \tfrac{1}{2}n(n+1)$$

(ii) $S_3(n) = 1^3 + 2^3 + 3^3 + \cdots + n^3$

The difference table for $S_3(n)$ is:

n	$S_3(n)$	$\Delta_1 S_3(n)$	$\Delta_1^2 S_3(n)$	$\Delta_1^3 S_3(n)$	$\Delta_1^4 S_3(n)$
1	1				
2	9	8	19		
3	36	27	37	18	6
4	100	64	61	24	6
5	225	125	91	30	
6	441	216			

$$S_3(n) = S(n_k) + \theta \Delta_1 S(n_k) + \tfrac{1}{2}\theta(\theta - 1)\Delta_1^2 S(n_k)$$
$$+ \tfrac{1}{6}\theta(\theta - 1)(\theta - 2)\Delta_1^3 S(n_k)$$
$$+ \tfrac{1}{12}\theta(\theta - 1)(\theta - 2)(\theta - 3)\Delta_1^4 S_3(n)$$

Again we may take $n_k = 1$ and $\theta = n - 1$, and so

$$S_3(n) = 1 + (n-1) \times 8 + \tfrac{1}{2}(n-1)(n-2) \times 19$$
$$+ \tfrac{1}{6}(n-1)(n-2)(n-3) \times 18$$
$$+ \tfrac{1}{12}(n-1)(n-2)(n-3)(n-4) \times 6$$

This involves a lot of calculation, which leads to the following result

$$S_3(n) = \frac{n^2}{4}(n + 1)^2$$

Note

There is a "trick" to simplify the calculation; put

$$S_3(n) = 0^3 + 1^3 + \cdots + n^3$$

i.e. begin with $n_k = 0$, and then we have

$$S_3(n) = 0 + 1\theta + 7\frac{\theta(\theta - 1)}{2} + 12\frac{\theta(\theta - 1)(\theta - 2)}{6}$$

$$+ \frac{6\theta(\theta - 1)(\theta - 2)(\theta - 3)}{24} \quad \text{with } \theta = n$$

$$= \tfrac{1}{4}\{n^4 + 2n^3 + n^2\}$$
$$= \tfrac{1}{4}n^2(n + 1)^2 \qquad\qquad \blacksquare$$

In your solution to Exercise 2 you will notice that the first differences of $S_2(n)$ are the squares of the natural numbers, and the function "square it" is a quadratic polynomial function; therefore $S_2(n)$ must be a polynomial of degree one higher — a cubic. Your solution also showed that the unique cubic polynomial that fits the values of $S_2(n)$ at $n = 1, 2, 3, 4$, is

$$\frac{n(n + 1)(2n + 1)}{6}$$

To be precise we would need to argue in the following way:
We have

$$S_2(n + 1) = 1^2 + 2^2 + \cdots + n^2 + (n + 1)^2$$

and

$$S_2(n) = 1^2 + 2^2 + \cdots + n^2;$$

it follows that

$$\Delta_1 S_2(n) = S_2(n + 1) - S_2(n)$$
$$= (n + 1)^2, \text{ so that}$$
$$S_2(n) = C(n) + p(n)$$

where $C(n)$ = cubic polynomial in n, and $p(n)$ = periodic function of period 1, i.e.

$$p(1) = p(2) = \cdots = p(n) \quad \text{(See Exercise 4.2.1.5)}$$

If we now put $C(n) = \dfrac{n(n + 1)(2n + 1)}{6}$, then $S_2(1) = C(1) + p(1)$, but $S_2(1) = C(1) = 1$, i.e. $p(1) = 0$ hence $p(n) = 0$. So that finally

$$S_2(n) = C(n) = \frac{n(n + 1)(2n + 1)}{6}$$

Consequently $S_2(n)$ must be equal to this polynomial not only for $n = 1, 2, 3,$ and 4 but for all positive integers, and we conclude that

$$1^2 + 2^2 + 3^2 + \cdots + n^2 = \frac{n(n + 1)(2n + 1)}{6}$$

4.3.4 Summary

In this part we showed that interpolated and extrapolated values of a tabulated function may be calculated by the Gregory-Newton Formula

$$g(x) = f(x_k) + \theta \Delta_h f(x_k) + \frac{\theta(\theta - 1)}{2} \Delta_h^2 f(x_k)$$

$$+ \cdots + \frac{\theta(\theta - 1) \cdots (\theta - n + 1)}{n!} \Delta_h^n f(x_k)$$

where

$$\theta = \frac{x - x_k}{x_{k+1} - x_k}$$

(with the usual proviso about the danger of extrapolation).

The formula is the basis of many which are used very widely in practical computation, especially in connection with a computer. (It is not, however, particularly suitable itself as alternative formulas can achieve the same degree of accuracy with considerably less calculation.) A second use of the formula is to deduce formulas for the sum of the elements in a sequence of numbers, such as the sum of powers of the natural numbers. These formulas will be used in a later unit on integration and are occasionally needed in other fields.

4.4 ERRORS

4.4.0 Introduction

This section gives another application of finite differences. We feel it is sufficiently important and interesting to include it here, but, since subsequent units do not depend on this section, you can omit it if you are short of time and due to get on with the next correspondence text, which is for *Unit 6*.

Up to now we have treated the tabular values as the exact values of the function at the tabular points. This is, however, an over-simplification. Tabular values are almost always inexact, if only because of round-off errors; moreover in all too many cases, occasional tabular values are not even approximately correct because of some blunder either in finding the value of the images of the function or in copying the numbers into the table. In this section you will learn how to recognize and allow for the effect of round-off errors when using a difference table, and how the difference table makes it possible, in favourable cases, to locate and even to correct a tabular entry that is wrong because of a blunder.

4.4.1 Blunders

We consider blunders first because their effect on the difference table is more dramatic than that of round-off errors. Here are two six-figure tables of values for the cosines of the numbers from 0.512 to 0.518 at a spacing of 0.001. One of the tables contains a deliberate wrong number, such as could arise from a copying error. By comparing the two tables you can see which tabular point has a wrong tabular value against it in one of the two tables; but can you tell which table is the wrong one?

Table I		Table II	
x	$? \cos x$	x	$? \cos x$
0.512	0.871 766	0.512	0.871 766
0.513	0.871 276	0.513	0.871 276
0.514	0.870 785	0.514	0.870 785
0.515	0.870 293	0.515	0.870 239
0.516	0.869 800	0.516	0.869 800
0.517	0.869 306	0.517	0.869 306
0.518	0.868 811	0.518	0.868 811

One way to find out whether Table I or Table II is the one with the error at $x = 0.515$ is to construct their difference tables (the decimal point is usually ignored in doing this):

Table I with Differences

| x | ? cos x | Differences | |
		First	Second
0.512	0.871 766		
		−490	
0.513	0.871 276		−1
		−491	
0.514	0.870 785		−1
		−492	
0.515	0.870 293		−1
		−493	
0.516	0.869 800		−1
		−494	
0.517	0.869 306		−1
		−495	
0.518	0.868 811		

Table II with Differences

| x | ? cos x | Differences | | |
		First	Second	Third
0.512	0.871 766			
		−490		
0.513	0.871 276		−1	
		−491		−54
0.514	0.870 785		−55	
		−546		+162 ...
0.515	0.870 239		+107	
		−439		−162 ...
0.516	0.869 800		−55	
		−494		+54 ...
0.517	0.869 306		−1	
		−495		
0.518	0.868 811		...	

In Table I the second differences are constant, so that the tabular values can be fitted by a quadratic polynomial in x; but in Table II the later columns of differences are very irregular, so that no simple polynomial gives any reasonable fit to the given tabular values. Since the graph of the cosine function is a fairly smooth curve, this is very strong evidence that Table II is the one that is in error, and that the value 0.870 239 given in Table II at $x = 0.515$ should really be 0.870 293 as in Table I.

Not only can we use the differences to tell whether or not there is a wrong value in a table, but we can often use it also to locate the wrong value and even to correct it. The method is an extension of a method that experimental scientists use. In making a series of measurements of some quantity at a succession of different times or of different values of some experimental condition such as temperature, it is standard practice to plot the results on a graph. If it then turns out that all the points but one lie on a smooth curve, the experimentalist takes this as evidence that a blunder was made in taking the corresponding measurement and if possible repeats the measurement to find out what went wrong. (If the measurement cannot be repeated there is a strong temptation to reject the anomalous measurement altogether, but what is really required is some explanation of why it is anomalous; it may not be in error at all, but may indicate a significant physical result!)

To see how the difference table can be used to detect wrong or anomalous values in the table let us assume that the blunder replaces the value that should be $f(x_k)$, in the table of f, by a wrong value which we denote by $f(x_k) + E$; thus E is the error introduced by the blunder into the tabular value for the tabular point x_k (see Table III).

Table III

x	f
...	...
x_{k-2}	$f(x_{k-2})$
x_{k-1}	$f(x_{k-1})$
x_k	$f(x_k) + E$
x_{k+1}	$f(x_{k+1})$
x_{k+2}	$f(x_{k+2})$
...	...

We can regard this as the table of a function that is the sum of f and an "error function" whose tabular value at x_k is E and at all the other tabular points is zero. In view of the fact that Δ_h is a homomorphism with respect to addition, i.e. that

$$\Delta_h(f + \text{error function}) = \Delta_h f + \Delta_h(\text{error function})$$

the difference table associated with Table III will be the "sum" of the difference table of f and that of the "error function", which is

Table IV

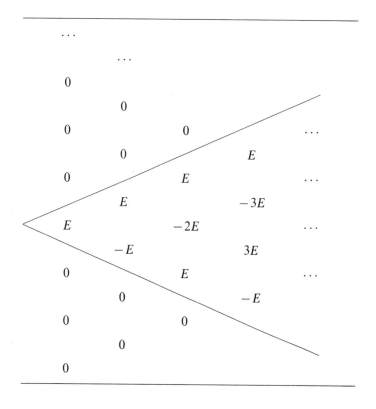

This shows that the error E affects more and more entries in each successive column of differences, the affected entries forming a triangular pattern. In any particular column, the largest effect occurs in the entries closest to the original wrong entry. (The values of the errors introduced in the rth column of differences are proportional to the coefficients in the binomial expansion of $(a - b)^r$.)

To illustrate the method for locating and correcting the wrong value let us apply it to Table II, which is repeated below with its difference columns.

Table II with Differences

x	? cos x	Differences		
		First	Second	Third
0.512	0.871 766			
		− 490		
0.513	0.871 276		− 1	
		− 491		− 54
0.514	0.870 785		− 55	
		− 546		+ 162
0.515	0.870 239		+ 107	
		− 439		− 162
0.516	0.869 800		− 55	
		− 494		+ 54
0.517	0.869 306		− 1	
		− 495		
0.518	0.868 811			

In the first difference column, it is difficult to disentangle the contribution of the error E from the contribution of the tabulated function, but in the second and third columns the contribution of the error E predominates, and the pattern shown in Table IV can be clearly discerned. The numbers in the second and third columns on Table II above can be fitted almost exactly to the differences of a single error E, shown in Table IV, if we take $E = -54$; for then Table IV becomes

Table V

0			
	0		
0		0	
	0		− 54
0		− 54	
	− 54		162
− 54		108	
	54		− 162
0		− 54	
	0		54
0		0	
	0		
0			

Thus from the differences of Table II alone we have strong evidence that its entry 0.870 239 at $x = 0.515$ is a wrong value of the form $\cos(0.515) + E$ with $E = -54$, and hence that

$$\cos(0.515) = 0.870\,239 + 54 \text{ units in last decimal place}$$

$$= 0.870\,293$$

This is indeed the correct value, as given in Table I.

Exercise 1

Exercise 1
(5 minutes)

Locate and correct the error in the table of cube roots below.

x	$\sqrt[3]{x}$
197	5.818 648
198	5.828 477
199	5.838 272
200	5.848 035
201	5.857 776
202	5.867 464
203	5.877 131
204	5.886 765
205	5.896 369
206	5.905 941

■

Solution 1

Solution 1

The difference table of the given values is

5.818 648			
	9829		
5.828 477		− 34	
	9795		+ 2
5.838 272		− 32	
	9763		+ 10
5.848 035		− 22	
	9741		− 31
5.857 776		− 53	
	9688		+ 32
5.867 464		− 21	
	9667		− 12
5.877 131		− 33	
	9634		+ 3
5.886 765		− 30	
	9604		− 2
5.896 369		− 32	
	9572		
5.905 941			

Here the third differences of the tabulated function are not quite constant, but the pattern is consistent with an error $E = +10$ which would contribute to the difference table as follows

			+ 10
		+ 10	
	+ 10		− 30
+ 10		− 20	
	− 10		+ 30
		+ 10	
			− 10

Thus the difference table indicates that the value 5.857 776 at the apex of the triangle is in error by + 10, and that the correct value is 5.857 766. ∎

4.4.2 Inherent Errors

Even if there are no blunders in the measurements or calculations whose results are recorded in a table, the tabulated numbers are still likely to be in error, both because of the limited accuracy of the process that produces them and because the numbers tabulated are rounded-off to some definite number of decimal places. In *Unit 2, Errors and Accuracy* we used the name *inherent errors* for all errors of this type. The purpose of this section is to show you how such errors limit the accuracy of calculations based on a difference table. We shall consider mainly rounding errors, but the same considerations apply to all inherent errors. As an example to illustrate the effect of rounding errors on a difference table, we consider the differences of a two-figure table of values of $\frac{x^2}{3}$ for $x = 31, 32, \ldots, 36$.

Table I

x	$\frac{x^2}{3}$	First	Second	Third	Fourth	
31	320.33					
		21.00				
32	341.33		0.67			
		21.67		−0.01		
33	363.00		0.66		+0.02	
		22.33		+0.01		−0.03
34	385.33		0.67		−0.01	
		23.00		0.00		0.00
35	408.33		0.67		−0.01	
		23.67		−0.01		
36	432.00		0.66			
		24.33				
37	456.33					

Since $\frac{x^2}{3}$ is a quadratic, we expect the second differences to be constant and the higher differences to be zero; but because of round-off errors the tabular values are not the exact values of $\frac{x^2}{3}$, and consequently the differences of the tabular values are not exactly constant in the second-difference column and not exactly zero in the later difference columns. When using difference tables, it is important to know whether the differences in the table reflect a real property of the tabulated function like the second differences 0.66 and 0.67 in Table I, or whether they are only differences of rounding-off error, like the third and fourth differences in Table I. In Table I the distinction is obvious, but is it so obvious in the following table?

Table II*

x	f(x)	First	Second	Third	Fourth	Fifth
0.25	0.247 404					
		9677				
0.26	0.257 081		−27			
		9650		2		
0.27	0.266 731		−25		−6	
		9625		−4		11
0.28	0.276 356		−29		5	
		9596		1		−7
0.29	0.285 952		−28		−2	
		9568		−1		1
0.30	0.295 520		−29		−1	
		9539		−2		2
0.31	0.305 059		−31		1	
		9508		−1		0
0.32	0.314 567		−32		1	
		9476		0		−2
0.33	0.324 043		−32		−1	
		9444		−1		
0.34	0.333 487		−33			
		9411				
0.35	0.342 898					

*The illustration is taken from P. Henrici, *Elements of Numerical Analysis*, (John Wiley 1964).

The differences decrease in size at first, then increase as the order of the differences gets higher. Can you say whether these changes represent a systematic trend or whether it is purely due to round-off errors? Such questions bring us near the border between our present subject, finite differences, and the problem of disentangling such systematic effects from the effects of erratic fluctuations such as round-off errors. The statistical approach to this type of problem may be touched on in the units on statistics, but here the methods of *Unit 2, Errors and Accuracy* are sufficient. We shall use these methods to calculate bounds for the errors in the difference table produced by rounding errors in the tabulated values. This will enable us to deduce that any entry in the difference table which is larger than this error bound must arise at least in part from a cause other than round-off error. This will help us to decide on the degree of polynomial with which we may reasonably approximate the tabulated function.

For the absolute error bound in $\Delta_h f(x_k) = f(x_{k+1}) - f(x_k)$ we add the absolute rounding-error bounds in the separate terms $f(x_{k+1})$ and $f(x_k)$, in accordance with the rules described in *Unit 2, Errors and Accuracy*. The absolute rounding-error bound in $f(x_{k+1}) - f(x_k)$ is therefore $\frac{1}{2} + \frac{1}{2} = 1$ unit in the last decimal place. For the absolute rounding-error bound in

$$\Delta_h^2 f(x_k) = \Delta_h f(x_{k+1}) - \Delta_h f(x_k)$$

we again add the absolute error bounds in the separate terms $\Delta_h f(x_{k+1})$ and $\Delta_h f(x_k)$. The calculation we have just done shows the absolute rounding-error bound of $\Delta_h f(x_k)$ to be 1 unit in the last place of decimals and that of $\Delta_h f(x_{k+1})$ is the same, by an analogous calculation. By the addition law for absolute error bounds, the absolute rounding-error bound in $\Delta_h^2 f(x_k)$ is therefore $1 + 1 = 2$. In the same way the absolute rounding-error bound of $\Delta_h^3 f(x_k)$ is $2 + 2 = 4$, that of $\Delta_h^4 f(x_k)$ is $4 + 4 = 8$, and, in general,

> the absolute rounding-error bound of $\Delta_h^r f(x_k)$ is 2^{r-1} units in the last decimal place.

Exercise 1

Exercise 1
(3 minutes)

Calculate the errors produced in a difference table by round-off if the round-off errors in the tabular values are alternately $+\frac{1}{2}$ units and $-\frac{1}{2}$ units in the last decimal place, and compare with the absolute error bound of $\Delta_h^r f(x_k)$, given above. ∎

Returning to the example considered in Table II we can now test the significance of the trend of the numbers in the difference columns. For instance, the absolute rounding-error bound of the fifth differences is $2^4 = 16$; consequently any fifth differences whose numerical value is less than 16 may be due purely to rounding error. We conclude that the tabulated fifth differences do not give any firm evidence about the nature of the tabulated function. We look for those of the difference columns in which the entries may not be *entirely* attributed to round-off errors.

Discussion

Exercise 2

Exercise 2
(2 minutes)

Which of the differences in Table II *are* appreciably different from zero (i.e. cannot be attributed entirely to rounding)? ∎

From the answer to this last exercise we can draw the conclusion that there is no point in trying to fit the tabulated values of the function in Table II with any polynomial of higher degree than a quadratic. If we

Discussion

tried to use any higher degree we would be adjusting the polynomial to the rounding errors and not to the function itself. The implication is that for interpolation in Table II a quadratic interpolation formula, such as the quadratic Gregory-Newton formula, given by Equation (4) of Section 4.3.2, gives the highest accuracy that this table can possibly yield.

Exercise 3

What is the degree of the optimum interpolation polynomial for interpolation in the following table? Use it to find tan (1.4975).

x	$\tan x$
1.495	13.1680
1.496	13.3447
1.497	13.5262
1.498	13.7127
1.499	13.9043
1.500	14.1014

Exercise 3
(3 minutes)

■

Solution 1

	First Diff.	Second Diff.	Third Diff.	Fourth Diff.
$\frac{1}{2}$				
	-1			
$-\frac{1}{2}$		2		
	1		-4	
$\frac{1}{2}$		-2		8
	-1		4	
$-\frac{1}{2}$		2		-8
	1		-4	
$\frac{1}{2}$		-2		
	-1			
$-\frac{1}{2}$				

The differences of the errors are seen to be doubled, in this case, at each differencing. So we see that with this choice of round-off errors we obtain the absolute round-off error bound of $\Delta_h^r f(x_k)$, i.e. 2^{r-1}. ∎

Solution 2

The first and second differences are definitely meaningful and *different* from zero. The absolute rounding-error bound of the third differences is $2^2 = 4$, thus any third differences whose numerical value is less than 4 may be due to rounding error. Thus we would consider the third differences *not* to be appreciably different from zero. ∎

Solution 3

x	$\tan x$	Differences			
		First	Second	Third	Fourth
1.495	13.1680				
		1767			
1.496	13.3447		48		
		1815		2	
1.497	13.5262		50		-1
		1865		1	
1.498	13.7127		51		3
		1916		4	
1.499	13.9043		55		
		1971			
1.500	14.1014				

For second differences the absolute error bound is 2 units in the last decimal place; therefore the tabulated second differences are significant. For third differences the absolute error bound is 4; therefore the tabulated third differences are not significantly different from zero. Hence the interpolation formula giving the best attainable accuracy without unnecessary work, is the one obtained by treating the third differences as zero, and it is therefore of the second degree.

By the Gregory-Newton formula,

$$\tan (1.4975) \simeq 13.5262 + 0.1865\theta + 0.0051\frac{\theta(\theta - 1)}{2} \text{ with } \theta = \tfrac{1}{2}$$

$$= 13.5262 + 0.0932 - 0.0006$$

$$= 13.6188 \qquad ∎$$

4.4.3 Summary

In this last part we showed how blunders lead to a difference table of the form

$$
\begin{array}{ccccc}
 & & & & E \\
 & & E & & \\
 & +E & & -3E & \\
E & & -2E & & \\
 & -E & & +3E & \\
 & & E & & \\
 & & & -E &
\end{array}
$$

which often makes it easy to detect and correct such blunders.

On the other hand, rounding-off errors of $\pm\frac{1}{2}$ in the last decimal place, lead to error bounds for successive differences of 1, 2, 4, 8 respectively. Hence, if we find the magnitudes of the differences beyond the rth do not exceed 2^{r-1} in the last decimal place, we can conclude that the function is a polynomial of degree r, with round-off errors, or, to be more precise, that there is no point in trying to represent the function by a polynomial of higher degree than r.

The methods of finite differences lead to methods for the interpolation and extrapolation of any continuous function and for the deduction of general formulas.

This concludes our consideration of finite differences — a subject of vital importance in practical computing, which also sheds an interesting light on the behaviour of functions in general and introduces ideas which will be taken up in later work on sequences, integration and differentiation.

Acknowledgements

Grateful acknowledgement is made to the following sources for material used in this correspondence text:

Texts

John Wiley and Sons Ltd, *Handbook of Engineering Fundamentals* by O. W. Eshbach, 1966, and *Elements of Numerical Analysis* by P. Henrici, 1964;
Cambridge University Press, *Science and Music* by Sir James Jeans, 1961;
The Rt. Hon. P. J. Noel-Baker, *The Arms Race* published by Oceana Publications 1956.

Illustrations

The Mansell Collection, photographs of Karl W. T. Weierstrass and Joseph-Louis Lagrange.

Unit No.		Title of Text
1		Functions
2		Errors and Accuracy
3		Operations and Morphisms
4		Finite Differences
5	NO TEXT	
6		Inequalities
7		Sequences and Limits I
8		Computing I
9		Integration I
10	NO TEXT	
11		Logic I — Boolean Algebra
12		Differentiation I
13		Integration II
14		Sequences and Limits II
15		Differentiation II
16		Probability and Statistics I
17		Logic II — Proof
18		Probability and Statistics II
19		Relations
20		Computing II
21		Probability and Statistics III
22		Linear Algebra I
23		Linear Algebra II
24		Differential Equations I
25	NO TEXT	
26		Linear Algebra III
27		Complex Numbers I
28		Linear Algebra IV
29		Complex Numbers II
30		Groups I
31		Differential Equations II
32	NO TEXT	
33		Groups II
34		Number Systems
35		Topology
36		Mathematical Structures